The Investment Behaviour of British Life Insurance Companies

J.C. DODDS

CROOM HELM LONDON

© 1979 J.C. Dodds
Croom Helm Ltd, 2-10 St John's Road, London SW11

British Library Cataloguing in Publication Data

Dodds, James Colin
    The investment behaviour of British life
    insurance companies.
    1. Insurance companies – Great Britain
    – Investments – Mathematical models
    I. Title
    332.6'725   HG8598
ISBN 0–7099–0058–9

Printed in Great Britain by
Biddles Ltd, Guildford, Surrey

CONTENTS

TABLES AND FIGURES

Tables

Figures

ACKNOWLEDGEMENTS

In presenting a study of this type, I must acknowledge my debt to the literature. My greatest thanks, however, go to my co-research colleagues in Sheffield who have been involved in the joint research work into models of the financial system and financial institutions which we have carried out over the past seven years; work which has been financed by the SSRC and the Esmée Fairbairn Charitable Trust. Professors George Clayton and Jim Ford have always given positive encouragement to me in all my work and in this present case, they have read all the chapters of a previous draft. This book is therefore dedicated to them.

I must also acknowledge the assistance I have received from a number of other sources, particularly the investment managers and others that I have talked to who have commented on some of my work. I feel I must single some of these out for special mention. B.H. Davies as well as providing useful insight into investment problems provided the data so that I could construct Figure 2.1 (a)-(c) in Chapter 2, J.F. Richards, R. Stonehill and D. Clayton likewise provided stimulating discussions and J.R. Hemsted gave up an inordinate amount of his time to give me the benefit of his long experience in investment management. In addition, I must extend a special thank you to Professor R.L. Carter, who read the entire manuscript and offered many valuable comments. Naturally I must claim responsibility for what has finally appeared and the errors and misinterpretations that may still remain.

The regression evidence was obtained using in the main two programs run on Sheffield University's ICL 1906 computer. One of these programs that we have used in Sheffield for virtually all our previous modelling work was written by Jon Stewart, late of the University of Manchester. I also used the TSP package from the University of Essex. The typing as usual has been excellently performed by Mrs Sheila Watts. She has the knack of coping with my handwriting. Mrs Muriel Burton assisted in some of the data analysis and proof reading.

My final acknowledgement must go to my wife, Carol, who over the years has had to endure the by-product of my work. She has always provided positive encouragement and in this case insistence that this particular piece of work be completed. In the meantime she also provided me with a son, James, who has also had to learn the (doubtful?) value of computer print out.

PREFACE

The modelling of the UK financial sector and financial intermediaries has become in recent years a popular research topic. A lot of impetus to this came from the work of J.M. Parkin (and others) on commercial banks (116) and discount houses (115), and D. Ghosh on building societies (68). All these studies used a simple Freund (65) utility function, and the present writer as part of a research team followed a similar strategy in a 9-sector financial model in 1972 (31). Our justification for building multi-sector and multi-asset models was that the various financial institutions were sufficiently different in their liabilities and assets held that their portfolio behaviour would differ. The cost-benefit analysis of such large-scale models involves the sacrifice of many of the behavioural aspects of this behaviour and we embarked on a strategy of attempting to study individual classes of financial institutions in more detail on a partial basis before placing them back into an even larger (10-sector) model. We did some preliminary work (and unpublished work on the banking sector) and subsequently we published our critique of existing models on building societies as well as presenting our own results in an input—output model. As life offices[1] and superannuation funds were included in our 10-sector model it became a natural topic for further research. In the event the present writer decided to focus attention on life offices *per se* and this present book is based on an unpublished PhD thesis presented at Sheffield University.

The literature available at the industry level included the work of G. Clayton (29) (30), R.L. Carter (25) (26), and the definitive work on the investment principles of life offices of G. Clayton and W.T. Osborn (33). Since then we have had one further industry study, that by P.J. Franklin and C. Woodhead (61) although that is not to be published until 1979 and we have not been able to take account of their work in this study. At the outset of our work therefore there were no econometric studies of their portfolio behaviour but since then we have had the work of T.M. Ryan (144) and the unpublished studies of A. Munro (110) and R.L. Carter and J.E.V. Johnson (27). Additionally, we have witnessed important changes in the sector itself with more statutory control and calls for greater supervision and control in financial markets. Indeed we still await the findings of the Wilson Committee

(168) which should provide a wealth of evidence and analysis of the present-day financial system.

Our objective in writing this book has been to set out critically the analytical base of the investment behaviour of life offices. We see this as a useful exercise in itself and as a means of providing guidelines for further work in this still neglected area. Our own econometric work, which is contained in Chapters 5 and 6, does not therefore claim to be the definitive work on life office investment behaviour. In Chapter 5 we have attempted to quote results that test the various hypotheses we have advanced in the discussions in earlier chapters. Inevitably those equations are only a small part of what we actually ran and although the choice was a difficult one to make, we have attempted to justify the estimations utilised. In other words we would argue that this is not just a regression exercise for the sake of achieving the highest fit. Our purpose has been to develop as far as possible models which appear to fit the facts and in the event, if predictive power is also taken into account as well as description and explanation, the models are a reasonable first step. Inevitably, with better data series we could have done more and even with the existing data there are many other areas which could be developed. We are therefore very conscious that there are many other important issues and problems which we could not take up and develop. We illustrate some of these in the final chapter.

In economics we know that there are (quoting from Joan Robinson) no 'knock-down' answers to a question and our feelings are well summed up in the following quotation from Lord Kelvin:

When you can measure what you are speaking about and express it in numbers you know something about it, but when you cannot measure it, when you cannot express it in numbers your knowledge is of a meagre and unsatisfactory kind.

McMaster University, Canada   J.C.Dodds
November 1978

Notes

1. We use the words life offices and life companies interchangeably throughout this study and of course 'we' is used throughout as the Royal 'we'.

This book is dedicated to
GEORGE CLAYTON and JAMES L. FORD

1 THE BUSINESS OF LIFE INSURANCE

1.1 Introduction

Insurance has been an important method by which the problem of risk in the world of business and in the life of the individual person has been met. Here we are using risk in the Knightian sense (93) in that there will be probability distributions accompanying the outcomes; and as G.L.S. Shackle has argued

> For the insurance company . . . probability provides knowledge. The number of accidents per year per thousand of insured may in many contexts be a fairly stable proportion, changing slowly and steadily as a consequence of social and technological evolution. Thus what is for the individual a non-divisible experiment can become in the hands of the insurance company part of a divisible one. It can be pooled with scores of thousands of others and thus the individual can exchange the certainty of a small loss (the premium on the policy) for the haunting possibility of a total one ((146) pp. 108-9).

Of course, we can distinguish many different forms of insurance contract; although in practice two main classes are recognised — 'general' insurance which covers all forms of insurance other than 'life' and is written on an annual basis (fire, auto, marine, household, etc.) and 'life' insurance which is usually a long-term one in that 'it provides cover against risk of death or of survivance; . . . [and] it provides an investment service involving guarantees of future capital security and long-term interest yield' (A.T. Haynes and R.J. Kirton (76) p. 141). Whilst not all policies, as we shall see, do combine protection and savings elements, the ability to mix these in various ways has given the life insurance contract great flexibility and thus accounts (in part) for the continual expansion in life business. Likewise the 'general' insurance area has expanded and there is continual innovation to produce policies which suit particular needs. But these modern-day conditions have taken a long time to evolve and we need to digress to cover some of the beginnings of 'insurance' to see how the foundations for its present success were laid. (For a comprehensive history of insurance see H.E. Raynes (129) (130) (131); also G. Clayton (30), and B. Supple (157). For a short account from 1880 see J. Johnston and G.W. Murphy (87).)

The history of 'insurance' in trade and commerce can be traced back to the fourth century BC and certainly it was well developed in Italy and some other European countries in the fourteenth century and whilst Britain was relatively late in developing the insurance contract (it is not until the sixteenth century that records are to be found), by 1570 – the date of the opening of the Royal Exchange – insurance contracts for marine risks were commonplace.

Two strands have been present in these early beginnings of life assurance. The first had its origins and basis in the concept that the hardship caused by death can be reduced or mitigated if a group of people are willing to pool their resources, so as to provide funds for the dependants of the deceased. This can, in fact, be traced back to the Anglo-Saxon period, continuing through the Middle Ages, and the trade guilds were an important force in this process. But the first office to open to the general public was 'The Society of Assurance for Widows and Orphans' which was founded in 1699. The objective of this society was to pay £500 on the death of each member out of the contributions of 5 shillings from each of the 2,000 members. Whilst the society only survived for twelve years, allegedly owing to the fact that full membership was not achieved, the principle behind the venture was adopted by the 'Amicable Society' in 1706 and this continued in business for over a century. The Amicable charged an annual premium of £6 4s 0d and the benefit paid, which once the society was firmly established, varied between £100 and £300, depended on the actual mortality experience. It is also interesting to note that evidence of 'health and habits' was required and that later an age entry barrier of 45 was introduced. Many other such schemes flourished over this period.

The second strand we can refer to was the recognition that life assurance could be carried out in a similar fashion to property insurance whereby temporary insurance cover was given and the first recorded instance of this is in 1548 (see Walford (164)) with the insurance of a Master with his ship. But the first term life policy *per se* for which records exist was that issued in 1583 on one W. Gibbons for one year for £382 6s 8d at a single premium of £8 per cent. Such policies became common in the seventeenth century although Daniel Defoe writing in 1697 did not entirely approve of them.

> Ensuring of life I cannot admire; I shall say nothing to it; but that in Italy where Stabbing and Poisoning is so much in vogue, something may be said for it, and on contingent annuities; yet I never knew the thing much approv'd of on any account (41).

Temporary assurance of this type continued well into the eighteenth century particularly with the establishment of supplementary charters for 'London Assurance' and the Royal Exchange in 1720. Companies wrote annual contracts (maximum £500 sum assured) at first, irrespective of age with a rate of premium being £5 or £5 5s; though they took the state of health very much into account.

These early beginnings of societies such as the Amicable – which gave in effect 'permanent' assurance – and the others which sold 'term' assurance were still a long way from writing the contracts which are used today. In fact, this period is often referred to as the 'hit and miss' or unscientific period of life assurance in that there was no formal actuarial basis for the calculation of premiums. Development in the late seventeeth century, however, provided a base to work on in that J. de Wit in 1671 wrote a report for private circulation on the value of life annuities in Holland (see F. Hendricks (80) for a translation) which indicates that he had a firm idea of mortality rate as it applied to a group of annuitants. In addition, work by W. Petty (122) on bills of mortality of London again increased knowledge of mortality. But it was Halley who, in a paper published in 1693, using the bills of mortality in the City of Breslau, pioneered the use of mortality tables in life assurance arguing that the price of assurance on lives 'ought to be regulated by the age of the person on whose life the assurance is made' (73, p. 105).

The most significant development in the eighteenth century was the work of James Dodson. He felt that the mutual protection as practised in earlier schemes had two main disadvantages. In the first instance most schemes had contribution rates set irrespective of age so that it was unfair on younger contributors. Secondly, in a year with fewer contributions and more claims there would be little to pay out to the beneficiaries. Instead he proposed a scheme in 1750 which would offer the benefit of level premiums over long-term contracts; but he could not get a Royal Charter. As an alternative he had to establish a mutual society of partners which in the event was not finally formed until 1762 (five years after Dodson's death) and became known as the Society for Equitable Assurance on Lives and Survivorship, owing its existence to one Edward Rowe Moore. It had four main innovations: (1) it was a self-capitalising mutual fund; (2) it offered level premiums that enabled people to continue insurance into their high-risk years without penalty; (3) it offered several types of policies; (4) payments were made in cash or annuities.

It is on the basis set out by the Dodson innovation (and the subsequent success of the 'Equitable') that the whole edifice of life assurance as it is today has been laid. The developments in actuarial science were applied in the Society for Equitable Assurance and we can usefully segment four stages in the history of life assurance from this date:

1762-99	application of scientific principles;
1800-1914	rapid growth of life assurance and development as financial institutions; consolidation and application of principles of life assurance to Friendly Societies, pension funds and social insurance and the emergence of insurance supervision;
1915-39	intermediate phase but questioning of principles underlying investment;
1940 to date	re-examination of fundamental principles, innovation and further growth.

Certainly by the end of the eighteenth century, life assurance was firmly established and other forms of insurance too were well developed, though the state had also found the need to legislate in 1774[1] and to introduce the concept of 'insurable interest' to prevent the gambling which had resulted from policies being issued against a number of contingencies such as the life of a highwayman. As H.E. Raynes (131) points out: 'There was absolutely nothing on which a policy could be opened that was not employed as the opportunity of gambling' ((131), p. 137).

The nineteenth century, as we have indicated, witnessed the growth and consolidation of life assurance business and although they were only one of many other types of financial institution that emerged and developed in this period (e.g. building societies), several factors have marked them out for a special place in the saving and investment processes over this period. Whilst their relative size and rapid growth are significant in themselves, their long-run outlook coupled with the need for markets to invest their accumulating funds have been critical factors in determining the principles which should govern the portfolio distribution in terms of the type of assets to hold. A.H. Bailey (5) was, in 1862, the first person to attempt to set these principles down into a coherent framework and since these early beginnings there has been an ongoing debate on the nature of investment criteria. However, we need to recognise that the growing needs of the life offices have also been influential factors in shaping the evolution of the capital market.

Increasingly the state has involved itself in establishing broad controls of life assurance and the regulating framework was established in Acts in 1867, 1870 and 1872. Requirements were established for minimum capital stock outstanding, a deposit of £20,000 to be made to the Paymaster General, separation of life assurance and accident insurance business records and the filing of accounts with the Board of Trade. But governments had recognised the difference between life assurance and other forms of saving by giving tax concessions to the policy-holders and these have been retained to the present time. Further legislation in 1909 retained the regulating provisions of previous legislation and companies were required to maintain a deposit provision for each type of insurance business in addition to the separate accounts: their disclosure in their balance sheets was also prescribed in much greater detail, but no separation of funds between ordinary life and industrial life assurance was required. This was later changed, however, by the Industrial Assurance Act whereby a separate deposit was to be made and a separate fund created for industrial life business.

It was the 1946 Assurance Companies Act (consolidating the 1909 Act and Acts of 1933 and 1935) which brought about the separation of insurance into long-term business: life assurance, industrial assurance and bond investment business; and general business: fire, motor, etc.; a distinction which is still used today. In addition, there was a third category of 'other'. The basis for this legislation had been laid in several pre-war committees, the Clauson (1924) and Cassel (1937) Committees, but a basic recommendation that these committees made for the segregation of assets of composite companies to protect life policyholders was not adopted. The Act set down a solvency margin for companies of £50,000 or one tenth of the general premium income of the company on the preceding financial year — whichever is the greater — and of course the 1948 Companies Act could bring about a compulsory wind-up. The provisions of the 1946 Act were consolidated into the 1958 Insurance Companies Act, but although these solvency margins were intended to prevent the entry of risky ventures, any company was free (except in the case of industrial life business) to transact insurance business. The 1967 Companies Act changed this, requiring potential new entrants to seek authorisation from the Department of Trade. In addition the Act had certain solvency provisions in that it gave authority to apply requirements to attempt to prevent insolvency. To be specific we can quote from the Act what these requirements were:

If it appears to the appropriate authority that the business of an insurance company, to which the principal Act applies, is being so conducted that there is a risk of the company's becoming insolvent, that authority may impose on the company all of the following requirements, namely

(1) . . . that the Company shall not make investments of a specified class and shall, before the expiration of a specified period (or such longer period as the appropriate authority may allow) realise investments of that class held by it immediately before the requirement is imposed.

(2) . . . that the assets of the company to a value not less at any time than the amount of its domestic liabilities at that time shall be maintained in the UK.

It was in the 1973 Insurance Companies Amendment Act that legislation was enacted to control directly the investment policies of life offices. Power was vested in the Secretary of State to ask for requirements that would restrict the previously enjoyed freedom, notwithstanding any risk of insolvency. These requirements were similar in form to those specified above. Subsequently draft regulations were introduced in the Insurance Companies (Valuation of Assets) Regulations in 1976. These were a more thoughtful and general set of regulations to extend control over the insurance industry so as to test their solvency and determine fairly stringent guidelines for the eligibility and value of assets. In the case of solvency, draft regulations envisaged a 10 per cent margin between the admissible value of the assets (at break-up value) and the value of the liabilities using a net premium discount rate based on the yield (running yield) currently being earned. These regulations, as they apply to liabilities, have not been endorsed[2] because they are not in line with EEC standards. Rules for the valuation of assets[3] are in force with some assets being inadmissible for solvency purposes. In the eligibility rules, limits have been set on an office's investment in any particular asset e.g. a building (5 per cent)[4] or a company security (7½ per cent). Life offices in the UK, however, still retain a considerable degree of freedom particularly with respect to their investment policy; something not found in other countries, for example, the USA.[5] We can however predict that the UK will be brought more in line with the practices in other countries, particularly the EEC.

1.2 Life Companies as Financial Intermediaries

The role of life companies in the saving and investment process leads us to examine life companies as financial institutions or, as they are now more often referred to, financial intermediaries. This is an area of study which has received a lot of consideration in recent years at both theoretical and empirical levels. In the case of the former we may cite the innovative work of D. Patinkin (117) and particularly J. Tobin and W.C. Brainard (163) (16) (17). For empirical work there has been a flood of work in the USA and to a lesser extent in the UK. However, relatively little work has been done on UK life company portfolio investment *per se*.

Financial intermediaries are transporters of capital by taking the savings of the surplus units and transferring this to deficit units who wish to borrow. Life companies in this process offer contracts for the future delivery of specific amounts of £ sterling in a prescribed manner through time in return for premium receipts. The contracts are essentially non-marketable (in terms of J.G. Gurley and E.S. Shaw (72) they are indirect debt) and therefore fairly illiquid. The life companies then purchase primary securities so as to at least honour the commitment made in the contract, lump sum or an income, but strive to achieve more than this.

Intermediaries are thus mobilisers of savings and whilst the transfer could occur without the need for intermediation, their existence tends

> to raise the levels of saving and investment and to allocate more efficiently scarce savings among alternative investment opportunities . . . They give lenders a wide variety of financial assets, particularly suited to their needs [and] . . . They enable spending units to escape the strait jacket of balanced budgets and to order their spendings more efficiently (J.G. Gurley and E.S. Shaw (72), p. 196).

They thus remove the direct contact which surplus and deficit units would have to have in the absence of intermediation. In other words, they bridge the gap so as to remove the hesitation and reluctance of dealing directly with one another which could normally result in surplus units either holding their savings as 'cash' with no return (but safe from risk of illiquidity and default) or as short-term capital-certain assets. To do other than this, surplus units would have to involve themselves in transaction costs associated with measuring such things as credit worthiness and, unless they were lending large sums, they would not be able to obtain a measure of diversification to reduce risk.

What intermediation does, as the quotation from Gurley and Shaw indicates, is to provide assets which savers wish to hold which will have liquidity and security attributes[6] thus permitting the reduction of cash holdings and so enlarging the secondary market for securities. But they can do this simultaneously without affecting the terms on which the funds are lent to borrowers. In fact, the terms available to borrowers may be more favourable to them. As J.R. Hicks (83) argues, there may be disparity in the preferred habitats of borrowers and lenders: borrowers 'will have a strong propensity to borrow long . . . most people . . . would prefer to lend short' (pp. 146-7). This simultaneous increase in borrower—lender satisfaction is referred to by P.F. Smith (154) as the transmutation effect and what it illustrates is that the liquidity of the whole economy can be increased therefore increasing the efficiency of money and credit. Whilst many institutions carry out the inter-mediary role, their specialism varies in terms of the liabilities they issue and the assets they hold. There are certainly key aspects which distinguish life companies from other financial institutions and the purpose of this study is to illustrate this by focusing on life companies themselves and to comment *en passant* on the differences and similarities that appear to exist between them and the other institutions that mobilise savings and invest these in the various financial markets in the UK and abroad.

We have discussed already the historical evolution of life assurance and we are now in a position to examine the life industry in a modern context. If we return to the quotation of Haynes and Kirton given earlier in this chapter then we can recall that this illustrated two of the important features of life assurance contracts (1) they can give protection so as to indemnify the policy-holder in the event of claim; and (2) the accumulation role they have in building up savings of the policy-holders. The fact that life offices do generate a substantial volume of saving is not surprising given that single premium policies and the level premium concept require the office to create a fund which can earn interest; and we illustrate the profiles of these funds in Chapter 2. The fact that the probability of death arises with increases in age involves a charge on policy-holders in the early years when net premiums exceed claims and expenses, but this is balanced in later years. Life offices also write annuity contracts[7] and although deferred annuities can be seen in the same light as the above, with immediate annuities (single premiums of funds accumulated elsewhere) the function of the office is not one of accumulation but of systematic liquidation with regard to life contingencies. So this is a third element to be added to the other two functions of indemnification (accepting mortality risk) and accumulation.

Haynes and Kirton used the word 'guarantee' and in this respect life offices are virtually unique in offering a guaranteed return[8] on a long-term basis by investing, in the case of most policies, a regular sum period by period. Only in the case of single premium policies could such a guarantee on the future nominal value be obtained outside the life contract, by purchasing government securities with a fixed maturity date so that the yield to maturity obtaining becomes the holding period yield. For a discussion of this financial yield see R. Frost (66). But even here two problems arise; separate cover would have to be arranged for the indemnification, and the coupon payments would have to be invested at unknown rates of interest.

We can illustrate the importance that life offices have in personal sector saving by means of Table 1.1 which indicates that their share of personal sector saving has fallen over the period, so that by 1976 they had almost 34 per cent (as measured by premium income) compared with 63 per cent in 1963. In Table 1.2 we give a comparison (based on total assets) between life offices and other financial intermediaries for the years 1963-76, which is our data period, and this illustrates that in absolute holdings of assets they are third in size to deposit banks, having been overtaken in recent years by building societies. The table also gives their growth rates for the period 1963-76. For an historical comparison, and further discussion, see D.K. Sheppard (148).

But as we have indicated already, there are many types of policies available and, indeed, there are various types of life offices. Taking the latter point first we can identify two broad classes: companies which are mutual (where the with-profit policy-holders 'own' the company) and proprietary (where there are shareholders); in addition, however, some offices write other types of insurance, often referred to as general insurance (marine, fire, accident, etc.). Additionally, offices which mix life and general business we refer to as composite offices. The second broad grouping is that of collecting friendly societies, though their significance in the size of funds they administer and policies they write is minimal.

If we concentrate attention on the 'companies' there are two main types of policies — ordinary and industrial (for a discussion of the recent history of industrial assurance see K.J. Britt (22)) where the main distinguishing feature is the method of collection (by agent in the case of 'industrial') and frequency of payment (weekly or monthly in the case of industrial). But it is important to analyse the different

Table 1.1: Saving with Life Insurance Companies, Annual 1963-76 (£ million)

	Premium income (1)	Personal savings (2)	(1) as a percentage of (2)
1963	1023	1624	63.0
1964	1109	1864	60.0
1965	1124	2184	51.5
1966	1212	2384	50.8
1967	1335	2340	57.1
1968	1455	2337	62.3
1969	1481	2579	57.4
1970	1676	3150	53.2
1971	2006	3416	58.7
1972	2596	4435	58.9
1973	2984	5727	52.1
1974	3336	7531	44.3
1975	3406	11179	30.0
1976	4202	12475	33.7

Source: The Life Offices Association, Associated Scottish life offices and the Industrial Life Office Association, National Income and Expenditure (The Blue Book).

types of policies since they will give rise to the different sizes of reserves and therefore different investment requirements and characteristics. Life companies write three basic types of business:

1. Life assurance contracts of which *whole* life policies offer protection, giving a high sum assured and in some instances 'with profits', with the premiums payable until death or about the age of 83; *term* insurance where protection only is given for a specified period; *endowment* (with and without profits) which can offer both saving and protection and the policies may be linked to an equity or property fund. In the case of the latter the separation between the saving and protection elements is made explicit in that either a separate fund is created with equity or property assets and run on unit trust principles, or the fund is notional, but with an explicit recognition of the underlying market values of the assets of the fund. The investor himself absorbs the investment risk and he receives the value of the units which

Table 1.2: Total Assets of Financial Institutions[a] (£ million) End Year
Selected Years 1963-76 and Growth Rates 1963-76 (Percentage)

Financial institution	1963	1968	1973 £ million	1976	1963-76 %
Deposit banks	9142	11741	23081	33677	10.9
Building societies	4005	7757	17709	28131	16.3
National savings	7933	8547	10449	12350	3.5
Pension funds	4636	7095	10852	14842	8.6
Unit and investment trusts	3134	6932	7912	8580	11.3
Life insurance companies	7425	11830	18125	25131	10.2
General companies	970	1334	2933	5564	14.7

Source: Financial Statistics, HMSO.

a. The deposit banks include the London clearing banks, Scottish and Northern Ireland banks and one or two other deposit banks (e.g. the Co-operative). The pension funds include public sector (funded schemes only), local authority and private superannuation funds and the valuation is in market value for local authority (end March each year) and private and for public sector after 1967. The market valuation is the cause of the fall in 1974 (likewise for unit and investment trusts). In life insurance, the public sector securities are at nominal values and the other assets at book values.

In comparing the total assets of the different institutions care must be exercised and the valuation problem is particularly acute for pension funds, unit and investment trusts, where the assets they hold are mainly marketable securities. Whereas in the main the assets of deposit banks and building societies are loans of one type or another and fixed in nominal values.

the savings element has purchased on maturity or when the policy is terminated by surrender or death.

2. Annuity contracts (*immediate* and *deferred*). Here business has increased dramatically mainly due to the introduction of guaranteed growth and income bonds. These became attractive by virtue of the tax position of an annuity fund. If the fund is paying out more in immediate annuities than is accruing in investment income to the fund, the income is free of tax and therefore can be passed on to the policy-holders. In addition, self-employed pension contracts have expanded following the tax concessions given.

3. The third class of business is that of group pension schemes. This business will be carried out using deferred annuities (with the group life element purchased via term assurance) and endowment policies where the maturity proceeds are used to purchase immediate annuities.

Surprisingly there are little detailed data available on the structure of life assurance business in the UK by policy types, although there are two official sources which provide, on an annual basis, the broad perspective. Yet even here it is difficult to reconcile the two sources to give a meaningful picture. This situation was also noted by J.R.S. Revell (134) who, for the period 1952-68, attempted to produce a more composite picture from a sample of 24 of the largest life offices. This thus provides another useful data source.[9]

Let us examine the two official sources. They are provided by the Life Offices Associations (LOA) and the Department of Trade and Industry (DTI). The LOA provide data on existing policies and new business and Table 1.3 summarises the data (1963-76) for life assurance business in force (UK and overseas) for annuities (immediate and deferred) and the sums assured and bonuses for ordinary life (including linked policies), industrial life and group pension schemes. In Table 1.4 we summarise the new business gained by life offices for our data period 1963-76. What these data indicate is the marked growth in single premium policies in the ordinary and industrial life business due to the growth of linked life assurance and the rapid growth in annuity business that we discussed earlier. Both were the result of innovation by the industry but despite this, it has not (as we saw in Table 1.1) increased the competitiveness of life companies in terms of their share of personal sector saving.

The Department of Trade and Industry (formerly the Board of Trade) do provide data on specified policy types (from the annual summaries supplied under the 1958 Act) on the basis of sums assured and the number of assurances or annuities, but these data are not strictly comparable with those published by the LOA. We quote the DTI data in Table 1.5 again for our specific data period[10] and we can note the split into policies 'with' and 'without' profits. In the case of the former the endowment contract would appear to be the dominant type of policy, though this dominance would appear to be weakening. For the 'without' profits policies the endowment contract has slipped to below the 'whole' life and the dominant policy type is 'other' which, whilst not delineated in the data series, includes annuities and term assurance. The data in this table only extend to 1973 as this is the latest available at the time of writing.

We shall examine the investment implications of these different classes of business and policy types in Chapter 2, but the fact that the policies do offer various different attributes — protection, guaranteed income until death, specific sum assured, etc. — implies that companies

Table 1.3: Total Life Assurance Business in Force — UK and Overseas[a]

Year	1963	1964	1965	1966	1967	1968	1969	1970	1971	1972	1973	1974	1975	1976
Life business in force (£ million)														
Annuities p.a. (immediate and deferred) (UK and overseas)	1030	1120	1220	1310	1410	1530	1660	1510 (179)[b]	1630 (187)	1820 (229)	2100 (293)	2410 (355)	2900 (482)	3510 (653)
Sums assured and bonuses – UK														
Ordinary life	10660	12410	14000	16100	18400	21400	24000	27800	33800	38800	45900	52600	62200	71500
Industrial life	4430	4940	5200	5450	5700	5940	6220	6450	6740	7110	7530	8050	8760	9560
Pension and life assurance schemes	4431	4892	5520	6260	6630	7350	8380	9320	10400	11800	13700	17500	22600	27500
Sums assured and bonuses – overseas														
Ordinary life	2540	2990	3380	3980	4950	5700	6150	6980	7440	9670	13900	16000	21100	28100
Pension and life assurance schemes	359	458	566	657	905	1100	1220	1410	1650	2010	2750	3460	5840	6900
Total sums assured and bonuses	22420	25690	28600	32447	36585	41490	45970	57960	60030	69390	83700	97600	120000	144000

a. Written overseas by UK offices and their wholly owned subsidiaries.
b. Figures in brackets refer to annuities overseas.

Source: Life Offices Association, Associated Scottish Life Offices and the Industrial Life Offices Association.

Table 1.4: Total New Business in the UK and Overseas

Year New business (£ million)	1963	1964	1965	1966	1967	1968	1969	1970	1971	1972	1973	1974	1975	1976
New yearly premiums			185	200	213	242	257	306	348	441	531	634	835	1050
	291	318	(15)	(13)	(23)	(26)	(21)	(37)	(43)	(54)	(77)	(87)	(144)	(183)
New single premiums and considerations for annuities	(11)	(24)	88	101	124	143	94	193	315	632	708	633	250	430
			(2)	(2)	(3)	(3)	(3)	(6)	(7)	(14)	(32)	(33)	(32)	(42)
New sums assured	4040	4920	5550	6490	7210	8340	9400	10900	13400	16000	19400	23400	31000	36600
	(689)	(826)	(840)	(934)	(1268)	(1345)	(1320)	(1810)	(2110)	(2640)	(3850)	(4690)	(6260)	(8270)
New annuities p.a. (deferred and immediate)	176	203	220	243	248	264	294	334	409	570	703	927	1070	1390
	(2)	(2)	(8)	(−8)	(19)	(21)	(10)	(39)	(48)	(58)	(65)	(67)	(122)	(202)

Note: The figures in brackets represent overseas business included in the total.

Source: Life Offices Association, Associated Scottish Life Offices and the Industrial Life Offices Association.

Table 1.5: Sums Assured Ordinary Business — Companies Established in the UK

	Policies without profits					Policies with profits				
	Whole life %	Endowment %	Joint %	Other %	Total £m	Whole life %	Endowment %	Joint %	Other %	Total £m
1963	9.8	26.4	0.1	63.7	8612	19.8	72.1	0.2	7.9	6053
1964	10.0	24.6	0.1	65.3	9673	20.3	71.9	0.2	7.6	6733
1965	9.7	20.4	0.1	69.8	11254	20.7	72.0	0.2	7.1	7738
1966	9.2	19.1	0.1	71.6	13161	21.0	70.8	0.2	8.0	8522
1967	9.3	17.1	0.1	73.5	15259	22.0	70.1	0.2	7.7	9696
1968	8.8	14.3	—	76.9	19521	22.1	68.9	0.2	8.8	11504
1969	8.7	11.6	—	79.7	21410	22.1	66.9	0.1	10.9	12197
1970	8.7	11.8	—	79.5	24527	22.6	65.8	0.1	11.5	13399
1971	9.7	11.0	—	79.3	29070	22.6	65.1	0.1	12.2	14861
1972	10.2	10.1	—	79.7	37337	23.3	63.5	—	13.1	17229
1973	11.2	9.7	—	79.1	43807	25.1	63.7	0.1	11.0	19986

Source: Annual Abstract of Statistics, HMSO.

are continually seeking to provide for the various needs of the public. This has involved a conscious policy of innovation and diversification (often linked to the available tax advantages) to maintain their share of total personal saving (something they have not been able to achieve consistently).

Various attempts have been made in both the USA and the UK to model the demand for life insurance. A.M. El-Mokadem (56), as part of his econometric study of personal sector saving in the UK, did attempt some specification of a possible demand function. But the main attempts have been in the USA and these have been more theoretical in their orientation and in particular we can cite the work of M.E. Yaari (170) (171), R.S. Headen and J.F. Lee (77) and to a lesser extent J.D. Cummins (39) and W.E. Nicholson (112). Clearly a knowledge of what factors are likely to be present in the demand for life assurance is important to life offices, both in terms of their marketing policies and their anticipated future new premium receipts. The wide-ranging nature of the business militates against any general or easy prediction although the growth in the group pension business (apart from new entrants) will be directly related to personal income. But having said that we need to derive estimates of national income which places us in the position of requiring macro-economic forecasts. This should be possible as there are a number of such models available, but as we have indicated, there has been no published systematic attempt to relate these macro model forecasts to the demand for insurance in the UK, though J.D. Cummins (39) in his econometric study of the life insurance sector in the USA used a forecast of this anticipated premium income that was derived from the Wharton Quarterly Model. The limits of this present study militate against exploring this particular avenue for the UK. However, we must make the obvious point that this is an important area for further work and certainly life investment officers have stressed to us that they continually attempt to predict cash flows. Indeed some go so far as to say that it is future cash flow that is important and that current market values and their fluctuations are irrelevant.

1.3 Outline of the Study

We have discussed the three functions which life companies perform in terms of indemnification, accumulation and liquidation and the type of policies that they issue which can combine these three elements. We have also indicated the significance life companies have in holding the savings of the personal sector and more particularly in their potentially influential role in capital markets, given the magnitude and rate of growth of funds to invest. Given their ability to lend in a wide variety of markets, the investment policy of life offices would appear to pose numerous and intricate problems for the administering of the investment process and for the economic, social and political impact this may have on financial markets. In this latter respect the Wilson Committee (168) was set up to examine the role of financial institutions in the City and their efficiency and effectiveness in providing funds for industry. Life companies are clearly a significant institution in this regard.

Our justification for examining life companies as a separate group of institutions is that only by such studies of separate groupings can we begin to understand the behaviouristic underpinnings of their portfolio behaviour. The *raison d'être* of institutions differs; hence the existence in developed financial systems of a large number of specialist institutions whose behaviour will be different. In approaching such a study we have attempted to achieve the following objectives:

1. Marshall the facts on the portfolio composition of life funds and their position in markets for securities in terms of their gross purchases and sales and net acquisitions.
2. Examine the principles on which life offices appear to operate in respect of investing the 'reserves' to meet future contingent liabilities. In part this can be gauged from observation of the actual displacement of funds and from the statements made as to what their objectives are and the constraints which limit and/or condition their behaviour.
3. Model their investment behaviour using the published data series.

Our approach throughout has been to treat life companies as an essentially homogeneous group, and the empirical estimation is based on published aggregate industry data. Whilst this has very clear limitations, given the wide disparity that exists between companies in terms of size, liability structure, attitudes to investment and portfolio dispositions, we feel that this study, by focusing on the industry,[11] is a logical first step in attempting to increase our understanding of the investment behaviour of life companies. The second step requires a micro-based study which is beyond the scope of this present work.

In attempting to achieve these objectives in Chapter 2 we analyse the sources and uses of funds of the life offices to illustrate the importance that the investment of policy-holders' reserves play in being able to guarantee the terms of the contract. We illustrate the portfolio composition in terms of holdings and net acquisitions and then we focus on the various markets in which they operate: government securities (fixed interest and ordinary shares), property, loans and mortgages so as to present the data on their acquisitions and disposals. In Chapter 3 we discuss what objectives life companies appear to have and the constraints that are operative. Our main focus of interest is the strategic decision-making process across asset classes rather than the switching within classes. We specify a typical asset demand equation which we develop in later chapters.

In Chapter 4 we present what empirical evidence there is for the UK which principally involves analysing one published study by T.M. Ryan (144) and one unpublished study by A. Munro (110).

Chapter 5 commences with an overview of the factors to be included in the estimation and then in Section 5.3 we follow a policy of estimating asset by asset equations which appear to explain the net acquisitions for the period 1963-74. The results presented represent only a small part of those actually run. In Chapter 6 we test the predictive power outside the sample period of these individual demand equations, then we attempt to fit these separate pieces into an integrated whole in terms of an overall model. Inevitably we cannot hope fully to explain behaviour, given the nature of the data and the changes which have occurred over our data period, but our purpose is to go some of the way to capture the key influences which appear to mould life office investment behaviour. The ultimate use that such an approach may have can be seen from the possible incorporation of some of the aspects of the model into improvements of the specification of the financial sector of macro-economic models. Such an undertaking is, however, beyond the scope of this study. In Chapter 7 we give an overall appraisal of the study and discuss areas for further work.

Notes

1. 'An Act for regulating Insurances upon lives and for prohibiting all such Insurances except in cases where persons insuring shall have an interest in the life or death of the person insured.'
2. See G.L. Barrow (8) for some discussion of these by the actuarial profession.
3. This can present some problems particularly with regard to mortgages. They can be regarded, on the one hand, as 'dead long' assets on the basis of the term lending and the fact that life offices have been reluctant to vary the rate of interest on them. Others regard them as 'dead short' on the basis that the average life of a mortgage is about 7–8 years and that if sufficient need arose (e.g. threat of insolvency) the rate of interest would be varied.
4. As a percentage of the life office's liabilities to its policy-holders, R.L. Carter

and J.E.V. Johnson (27) however, make the point that these limits can be exceeded by the use of 'free reserves'.

5. See K. Borch (14) for a discussion of the supervision of insurance companies in the USA.

6. As well as security and yield the intermediaries may offer other services such as financial advice, safe custody facilities, access to loans (for example a life insurance policy may carry with it a right to borrow against the surrender value).

7. Some of these policies may be for group pension schemes and whilst the majority of pension schemes are based on annuities, some are also operated through endowment policies, the proceeds of which are used to buy an annuity.

8. Some commentators would argue that this guarantee should implicitly cover the underlying rate of inflation, though this is a view not held by most life officers. We return to this point in Chapter 3.

9. J.R.S. Revell (134) estimated that for 1968 the total group pension fund (annuities, endowment and term policies) accounted for about 50 per cent of the total ordinary branch fund for UK business with premiums accounting for about 40 per cent of premium income.

10. The DTI data appear with a considerable time lag so that we cannot supply at the time of writing, data for 1974-6. For a discussion of life office returns to the DTI which include life office investment, see A. Ford (59).

11. We do however recognise the aggregation problem in that we are assuming that all the life offices behave in the same way and form the same expectations of the returns likely to ensue from investing in the various assets. Aggregation is the *sine qua non* for formulating models of the type we discuss in this study. But the fact that investment managers often keep a close watch on one another produces a tendency for many offices to do the same thing at the same time. Whilst this does exaggerate swings in the market it does give some support for taking the industry 'as if' it represents a consensus within individual offices.

2 THE FLOW OF FUNDS THROUGH THE LIFE INSURANCE SECTOR

2.1 Introduction

In this chapter we wish to focus on the activities of life offices as financial institutions. We have seen in the previous chapter their respective growth in terms of the personal sector saving they claim, and now we wish to cover the results of their activity in terms of their revenue and expenditure (sources and uses) and the essential link this has with the balance sheets of life companies.

The provision for future claims represents the liabilities which life offices have to discharge by means of their investment policy. These liabilities are not homogeneous and the wide range of different insurance contracts which are available, their length and the guarantees given, are three factors which distinguish their liabilities from those of other financial institutions. But just as their liability structure differs markedly from other financial institutions, so too does their asset structure since the assets they hold to back those liabilities extend to virtually every financial market. To illustrate the differing asset structure we need to cover both the stock and flow position of life offices (interpreted here as net acquisitions) as well as their gross trading (purchases and sales) in markets *vis-à-vis* other market participants. Our justification for this is twofold. In the first place simply to concentrate on net trading *in vacuo* is to neglect a dimension of life company investment behaviour, namely, its buying and selling. Secondly, as investment policy and action takes place within the context of financial markets of which life offices are only one (albeit in some markets, the main) investor, to neglect these market considerations may be to omit from discussion an important factor shaping price in the investment behaviour of life offices.

Our schema in this chapter is therefore to analyse the sources and uses of funds (Section 2.2); in Section 2.3 we present the published data on the trends in life insurance company investments both in terms of their portfolio holdings and their net acquisitions. In Section 2.4 we discuss the various characteristics of the assets life offices invest in to derive some *a priori* assessment of their relative substitutability/ complementarity. Section 2.5 we devote to a detailed analysis of the role of life companies in financial markets with respect to their

32

holdings, trading and net acquisitions. The purpose of this exercise is to derive some measure of their possible dominance in some markets as well as to assess the overall trends, particularly with respect to turnover. Our discussions in this chapter do extend over a wide field and do involve the use (necessarily in our view) of many tables (including some in the Appendix) so that in Section 2.6 we give an overall conclusion of the main points we feel we have made in the previous sections.

2.2 Sources and Uses of Funds

Sources of Funds

We have illustrated earlier in Chapter 1 the role of life insurance companies have in marketing policies which offer protection and/or saving to the public. The life insurance contract has proved such a flexible instrument that it is not surprising that the growth noted earlier in life insurance assets has occurred. The major sources of funds are the premium payments (including considerations for annuities) on the policies in force. This is well illustrated in Table 2.1 where for the period 1963-76 premium payments accounted for nearly 70 per cent some years of the sources of funds, falling to 59 per cent in 1976. Investment income accounts for the majority of the remainder and the item 'other income' includes such items as currency adjustments for overseas business and for the revaluation of assets. The premium income is made up of two parts: (1) the continuation of existing policies; and (2) the generation of new policies. Some of the latter will be single premium policies whilst others will produce a flow of premium receipts over the life of the policy which could extend to 50 years or more (on a whole-life policy). Even if no new policies were to be issued, the total funds under the control of life companies would still continue to grow (*ceteris paribus*) by virtue of the continuing payments of premium.

The flexibility of the life insurance contract noted earlier allows companies to mix the protection and savings elements. Over the period under review many new types of policies have been issued in response to changing consumer preferences which in part are a response to tax changes, higher interest rates and the increasing rate of inflation. The industry has thus been a vehicle for innovation by continually diversifying its product line — an essential strategy to ensure long-run growth.

If we examine the data on premium income in more detail we can notice two main trends. In the first place, annual growth has been volatile as illustrated in Table 2.2. In 1965, for instance, the growth rate was down to just over 1 per cent (as in 1969) yet by 1972 it was 29 per

Table 2.1: Sources and Uses of Funds — Life Insurance Companies, 1963-76 (£ million)

	1963	1964	1965	1966	1967	1968	1969	1970	1971	1972	1973	1974	1975	1976
Sources														
Premium income	1023 (69)[a]	1109 (68)	1124 (65)	1212 (65)	1335 (63)	1455 (63)	1481 (61)	1679 (64)	2006 (63)	2596 (65)	2984 (62)	3336 (67)	3386 (60)	4202 (59)
Investment income (gross of tax)	447	507	576	629	690	759	828	911	1007	1125	1339	1574	1830	2231
Other income	13	18	23	12	82	90	104	43	192	273	500[b]	95	530	694
Total	1483	1634	1723	1853	2107	2304	2413	2633	3205	3993	4822	5006	5746	7127
Uses														
Total payments to policy-holders	548	599	661	768	845	932	1073	1176	1317	1456	1627	1972	2188	2559
UK taxation	62	71	85	95	94	104	110	116	124	118	114	133	138	168
Management expenses (including commissions)	182	198	214	234	260	283	306	351	422	484	598	721	853	1030
Transfer to shareholders	15	15	20	15	24	27	28	26	43	32	44	50	56	76
Provisions for future claims	676	751	741	739	882	956	896	963	1278	1863	2435	2121	2518	3286

Notes: Total 'uses' of funds does not sum to the total of 'sources' due to rounding error and for the years 1971-4 due to the exclusion of sums added to life and annuity funds from policy-holders' reserves.
a. Figures in brackets are premium income expressed as a percentage of total sources of funds.
b. This figure is particularly high due to the acquisition of overseas subsidiaries.

Source: The Life Offices Association, Associated Scottish Life Offices and the Industrial Life Offices Association.

Table 2.2: Percentage Annual Rates of Growth of Sources and Uses
of Funds of Life Companies: 1963-76

	Sources		Funds of life companies		Uses
	Premium income	Investment income	Total payments to policy-holders	Management expenses	Provision for future claims
	%	%	%	%	%
1963	12.3	11.2	4.6	9.0	21.4
1964	8.4	13.4	9.3	8.8	11.1
1965	1.4	13.6	10.4	8.1	−1.3
1966	7.8	9.2	16.2	9.3	−0.3
1967	10.1	9.7	10.0	11.1	19.4
1968	9.0	10.0	10.3	8.8	8.4
1969	1.8	9.1	15.1	8.1	−6.3
1970	13.4	10.0	9.6	14.7	7.5
1971	19.5	10.5	12.0	20.2	32.7
1972	29.4	11.7	10.6	14.7	45.8
1973	14.9	19.0	11.7	23.6	30.7
1974	11.8	17.6	21.2	20.6	−12.9
1975	1.5	16.3	11.0	18.3	3.2
1976	24.1	12.2	17.0	20.8	17.0

Source: The Life Offices Association, Associated Scottish Life Offices and the
Industrial Life Offices Association.

cent. This cyclical movement in growth has also the second trend,
that of variable growth in the total sources of funds. This is to be
expected, of course, as Table 2.1 has illustrated that premium income
is the major 'source' of funds. To explain therefore the variable growth
of the total sources requires us to examine the component parts with
particular reference to premium income. This we do in Table 2.3.
Premium income is derived, as we saw in Chapter 1, from three main
types of life business: life assurance contracts (whole life and endowment), annuities (immediate and deferred) and pension and life assurance schemes. The data we presented there illustrated the relative
importance of those three types with respect to yearly premiums and
single premiums and these trends are confirmed in Table 2.3. What
we noted was the marked growth in recent years in 'single premium'
policies and considerations for annuities of various types. The growth

Table 2.3: Details of Premium Income: 1963-76 (£ million)

| | Ordinary life and annuity funds | | | | Other[a] | Industrial branch | Linked life[b] |
| | For assurances | | For annuities | | | | |
	Yearly	Single premiums	Yearly	Single premiums			
1963	454 (61)	9 (2)	188 (23)	152 (5)	—	220	—
1964	501 (70)	11 (2)	207 (24)	160 (6)	—	230	—
1965	542 (80)	10 (2)	223 (26)	107 (4)	—	241	—
1966	591 (92)	12 (2)	238 (22)	117 (4)	—	253	—
1967	646 (111)	13 (3)	266 (24)	147 (4)	—	263	—
1968	698 (126)	16 (3)	281 (28)	184 (5)	—	275	—
1969	743 (135)	14 (3)	309 (30)	129 (7)	—	286	—
1970	813 (149)	21 (5)	338 (30)	195 (8)	14	298	66
1971	917 (165)	120 (4)	373 (32)	264 (9)	17	312	86
1972	1030 (200)	366 (11)	436 (41)	407 (12)	22	331	92
1973	1230 (296)	372 (19)	503 (43)	494 (30)	21	356	121
1974	1390 (351)	232 (25)	644 (63)	655 (45)	24	382	168
1975	1530 (410)	214 (27)	810 (74)	392 (56)	28	418	182
1976	1900 (520)	235 (22)	1070 (126)	499 (76)	40	462	224

Figures in brackets represent overseas business included in the total.
a. From permanent health and capital redemption business.
b. Included in ordinary life — for assurance — yearly.

Source: The Life Offices Association, Associated Scottish Life Offices and the Industrial Life Offices Association.

of single premium business gives the life offices greater uncertainty than would the contractual payments on whole life, endowment policies and the like. In consequence, to maintain the rate of growth of this type of business requires individuals to shift out of other assets held in the financial system; something they may not always be willing to do. Even 'linked' policies can cause uncertainty as to the future growth of new business since they are directly geared to the property and equity markets. In bullish market conditions we might expect new business to expand and in bearish markets the converse. Though this conjecture requires more systematic analysis.

We also indicated that the different types of policies gave rather different mixtures of protection and saving with savings being low in the case of policies for protection and high in endowment contracts. This savings element generates funds for long-term investment and given the level premium system whereby the policy-holder overpays in the early years when mortality is low. The fund can also grow by virtue of the interest payments. If we take the endowment contracts as an example, then, although there is a level premium, there are two constituent parts of this to cover the different risks in the endowment contract. In the first instance, if only a relatively small amount has to be put aside for death cover, then the major part of the premium can go into the fund. But, as time progresses, increasingly claims on the contract require more provision for death and consequently less can enter the fund. This trend continues until the policy matures at the selected period and the combination of premium income and interest earned on the fund are sufficient therefore to pay off the claims at maturity. But this 'loading' of the premium element, so that in the early currency of a policy more is invested in the fund than is required to meet current claims in those years, means that those who do survive benefit from the contributions (and compound interest on them) of others. We can illustrate this for an endowment policy in Figure 2.1 (a), where we can note that the fund rises steadily until the policies mature.

The level premium concept is the same for whole life and annuities[1] though the profiles of the fund are rather different. For whole-life policies (see Figure 2.1 (b)) the fund grows until claims exceed interest earnings and assets have to be realised to pay the increasing mortality rate so that the fund declines. In single premium policies and annuities, the fund is created at the start and in the case of annuities the fund is reduced by the annual payment – this is shown in Figure 2.1 (c).[2]

Of course a life fund will consist of many different types of policies taken out at different dates so that these various profiles will be mixed

Figure 2.1 (a): Endowment Assurance

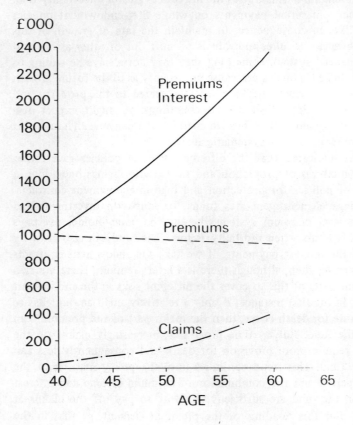

£000

Premiums
Interest

Premiums

Claims

AGE

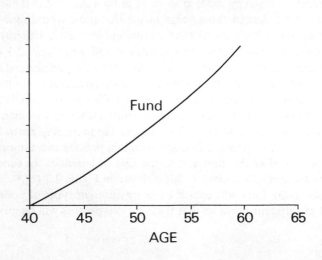

Fund

AGE

Figure 2.1 (b): Whole Life Assurance

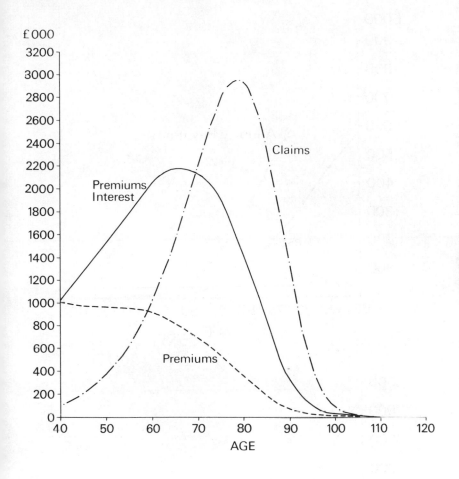

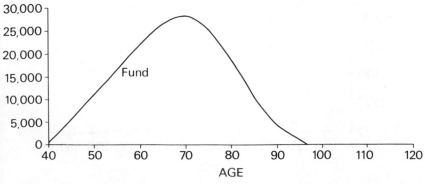

Figure 2.1 (c): Annuities

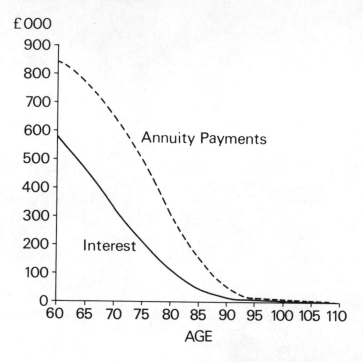

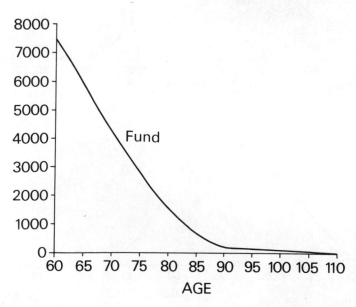

together: if there is a significant change in the types of policies, then this will change the nature of the fund created and the requirements of 'cash outgo' which itself may well condition the type of investment policy undertaken. We shall return to this issue in Chapter 3. The premiums are fixed by companies at the outset of the policy on the basis of calculations of expected mortality and an average rate of interest expected to be earned over the duration of the policy.[3] The underlying economic situation may change thus affecting the ability to earn the assumed rate of return and of course mortality experience may also change. The level premium system thus does have some dangers in it and to safeguard policy-holders companies have to be valued (using up-to-date information) every three years to ensure that assets cover liabilities.[4] The valuation is done by using the latest mortality figures which will give the actuary the incidence of claims with respect to the receipt of premiums. He discounts each annual stream back to the present using an average expected or assumed rate of interest as the rate of discount. The fact that companies do assume an expected rate of return in their calculations of premium then implies that this is in a sense the cost of capital (what we refer to later as c_i^p) or the cost of liabilities (policy reserves) which the companies hold on behalf of their policy-holders. So that this is analogous to the rate of interest payable on deposits with banks, building societies and other financial institutions. The differences are that the assets (the policy reserves) are not immediately encashable and the rate of interest calculated on the policy is not paid out, but is internal (and compounded) to the fund.

Whilst each life company must earn this return to meet its contractual liabilities,[5] they will normally have 'cushions' which allow them to absorb adverse changes in the assumptions made. Many actuaries in the past have erred on the side of caution in writing the policies and have left a margin between the expected value of investment return and the return they have built into the policy. Additionally they may even make a loading allowance in the mortality and operating expense elements of the form we have discussed already. These cushions are to be regarded as 'revenue' surpluses as they lead to an excess of income over outgoings and this can be divided among the various interested parties. If there are shareholders, they can benefit in the form of dividends; present (with-profit) policy-holders[6] can benefit by additions to reserves to be paid out in bonuses, usually reversionary bonuses. Alternatively premiums could be reduced. But in addition to this revenue surplus there may be a 'capital' surplus due to the fact that the asset valuation in the balance sheet is below the realised or realisation price on the market. This is particularly significant with equity and property holdings. Some of this surplus has in the past been used as a reversionary bonus and as this is a guaranteed bonus it is necessary to increase the value of assets to match the increase in liabilities. The remainder has been used as a terminal bonus which therefore gives more flexibility to the company. We can characterise the operation described above in terms of a single formula which equates the cost of capital — to a life company, based on the approach taken by J.D. Cummins (39).

$$p_i = \sum_{t=1}^{T} M_{i_t}^r (1 + c_i)^{-t} \qquad (2.1)$$

where the p_i are gross premiums which are paid on the ith block of policies at time $t = 0$, the date of purchase of the policy.[7]
$M_{i_t}^r$ represents the realised cost (in period t) in the ith block.
c_i the cost of capital for the ith policy block.
T the length of planning horizon of the company dictated by the ith policy block.

In fact we can subdivide the cost of capital c_i into two parts so that

$$c_i = c_i^p + c_i^n \qquad (2.2)$$

where c_i^p is the average rate of interest used to calculated the premiums, and
where c_i^n is the net cost of capital exclusive of c_i^p.

We have already referred to c_i^p but the c_i^n requires a little more explanation. If the other assumptions (mortality experience and expense costs) were to be realised (R.E. Beard (10) discusses the problems underlying random and systematic fluctuations of the actual from the implied experience), the company must earn c_i^p to break even. But, as we have already stated, the return that is used to calculate the premiums may be less than that which the actuaries/investment managers realistically feel they can achieve and the margin can be used for profit and other contingents. With the other hidden cushions available to companies, the overall cost of capital, c_i, could in fact be negative if c_i^n outbalances c_i^p, indicating that the company is making an underwriting profit. The converse would be the case if c_i^n were positive.

To make the analysis more realistic it is possible to introduce different policy blocks and to calculate the mean $E(c_i)$ and variance $\sigma^2(c_i)$ of the ith policy block as well as the covariance with other blocks so that we could have:

$$E(c) = \sum_{j=1}^{n} x_i E(c_i) \qquad (2.3)$$

where x_i is the proportion of liabilities in the ith block;

and

$$\sigma^2(c) = \sum_{i=1}^{n} \sum_{j=1}^{n} x_i x_j \, \sigma(c_i c_j) \qquad (2.4)$$

(where $\sigma(c_i c_j)$ is the covariance of the costs of capital between the ith and jth policy blocks.

Life companies can, as we have seen, introduce new policies and vary sales of the existing policies. Some offices in fact specialise in the types of policies they write. But if a significant change in product mix is required, then a promotion policy via advertising has to be followed or changes made in commission rates and premium rates. For example it could be possible to increase the sale of annuities almost overnight, by giving more favourable terms than their competitors; though this advantage may be only transient by virtue of the other companies following suit.

In writing contracts on which specific assumptions have been made with regard to mortality experience, management expenses and the rate of return one has to expect deviations from these. Whilst such similar changes would, in the case of most other financial institutions, produce a change in their operating behaviour and interest rate structure, as life companies can take the long view, they tend not to adjust their cost of capital. At the time of the Dalton Cheap money policies, however, there were fears expressed that companies would not be able to meet the c_i^p written into the policies already contracted and this would have caused c_i^n to increase. Since that time, with the progressive increase in the structure of interest rates, the c_i^p has been raised, but only after a lag. If mortality experience were worse than expected (and this is of course totally exogenous to the company), this would increase c_i so that this 'risk' is in part insulated by c_i^n. If the expenses element deviates from that built into policies, say by inflation, this again would cause an increase in c_i and this is a problem which has become particularly acute in Britain with the abnormally high rates of inflation in recent years. For a discussion of the experiences of life offices see E.S.W. Dyson and D.W. Elphinstone (53). Table 2.2 indicates the percentage annual rates of growth in these management expenses and they are substantially higher than those operative a decade previous. Two other possible causes are surrenders and policy loans in excess of that expected and we discuss these items in our coverage of uses of funds.

Uses of Funds

The premiums and investment income which flow into life companies, as we have seen, are used to meet claims and surrenders (Table 2.5 gives a detailed coverage of these payments to policy-holders), and to provide for future claims by means of building up policy reserves. These reserves are the liabilities of the companies as they are the result of the savings element in the level premium process discussed earlier. These reserves then illustrate the intermediary role of the life companies in that they represent the indirect assets (i.e. not marketable) held by the personal sector, allowing insurance companies to produce primary securities (in terms of Gurley and Shaw (72)); securities which households could purchase for themselves but which are less desirable to them. In fact, direct investment by the personal sector in stock exchange securities continues to decline illustrating, perhaps, the preference for more indirect debt.

Table 2.4: Revenue Account

Life assurance and annuity fund at beginning of year	F_0	Claims by death and maturity	C
Premiums	P	Surrenders (including surrender of bonus)	S
Annuity considerations	A	Annuity rents	R
Gross interest $I' = I + T$ Less income tax T		Expenses (including commission)	E
Net interest	r	Life assurance and annuity funds at end of year	F_1
Total	X	Total	X

Source: H.F. Fisher and J. Young (58).

To illustrate the essential linkage between the revenue accounts and the balance sheet accounts of the life offices, it is useful for us to summarise the sources and uses of funds in one table by giving a simplified revenue account, which summarises the total income and outgoings for the year. The fund at the end of a year $(F_1) = F_0 +$ (Income − Outgoings) and the increase in the fund period by period represents an accumulation of cash and in some versions of income and outgoing statements, it may be represented as a transfer to policy reserve and/or provision for future claims. This is the savings elements and it has been an extremely volatile element in growth terms as Table 2.2 indicated. Of course only a small part will be held in the form of 'cash' and therefore this represents the new funds available for investment[9] to back the sums assured (and future bonuses) and annuities (immediate and deferred) which life offices will have to meet in future years. We will wish to discuss the impact this may have on investment policy in Chapter 3.

Life tables are of course available to plot expected mortality so as to assess the incidence of claims on policies, and in fact claims are fairly predictable. But we cannot ignore the other uses of funds which have to be deducted before we arrive at the net inflow available for investment. For instance the expenses of operating the office (an increasing item as we have seen in these inflationary times) have to be met and these have been termed as 'friction' costs by J.D. Cummins (39) in that they represent the inescapable costs of intermediation. The taxes on investments are also inescapable, though companies are in a favourable position here, as we have already illustrated with regard to their annuity funds.

Two items in the 'uses' statement which companies find difficulty in predicting are 'policy loans'[10] and 'surrenders'. S. Wynn (169) estimated that 16 per cent of new *industrial* policies were forfeited within a short period and that most policies were eventually surrendered or forfeited. F.D. Patrick and A. Scobbie (118) estimated, on 1965 data drawn from a sample of five *ordinary* life companies, that rates of forfeits and surrenders were 6 per cent in the first year, 23 per cent in the first five years and 33 per cent in the first ten years. The data given in Table 2.5 indicate that surrenders have shown a large increase over our data period, with particularly large surrenders in 1969, 1973, 1975 and 1976. There are 'claw back' arrangements on the tax relief on policies if cashed in before a specified period but it is clear that many policy-holders do regard their accumulated bonuses as an encashable asset. Many policies carry a 'loan option' after a number of years when the loan is usually based on the surrender value of the policy. In fact, policy loans represent 'disintermediation' and whilst these are an asset item, they are included here in that companies have very little option in granting these loans. What is important is for companies to attempt to forecast both surrenders and policy loans as they are both paid out

Table 2.5: Payments to Policy-holders: 1963-76 (£ million)

	1963	1964	1965	1966	1967	1968	1969	1970	1971	1972	1973	1974	1975	1976
Death claims	141	148	162	175	180	201	216	236	249	283	317	363	401	460
Maturities	200	206	217	268	298	312	343	362	398	423	455	490	566	724
Annuities	69	89	106	119	135	159	178	199	220	252	298	354	412	464
Surrenders	84	92	108	123	141	160	198	214	249	275	348	523	513	619
Refunds (under[a] occupational pension schemes)	42	49	52	64	67	74	85	97	109	123	157	176	225	195
Bonuses in cash and in[a] reduction of premiums; other payments	12	15	16	19	24	26	52	68	92	100	45	66	66	96
Total payments made to policy-holders	548	599	661	768	845	932	1072	1176	1317	1456	1620	1972	2188	2559

a. Relates to ordinary branch business only.

Table 2.6: Simplified Balance Sheets for Life Companies

Yearly balance sheet			
Liabilities		**Assets**	
1 Shareholders' capital if any	SC	Mortgages, loans	
		Stock exchange, investments less reserves:	VA
2 Capital reserves (if any)	CR	Fixed interest	
3 Life assurance and annuity fund	F_1	Ordinary shares	
		Property	
4 Reserve fund	RF	Cash and deposits	
	$\overline{VA}$		$\overline{VA}$

Valuation balance sheet			
DR		**CR**	
To value of liabilities	VL	By life assurance and annuity fund	F_1
To surplus (if any)	S	By deficiency (if any)	D
	$\overline{F_1}$	* assuming D = 0	$\overline{F_1}^*$

of current income. But 'surrenders' are in a sense more of a problem in that the surrender value is based on underlying assets which are backing the policy and which may therefore have to be sold to meet this outflow. Alternatively, and more probably, both loans and surrenders could, if they were above the limits expected, be paid out of any liquid assets inherited from a previous period, but this would then limit the use of liquid assets for other investment purposes: there are as we have seen in Chapter 1, no statutory liquidity requirements of the type imposed in banks. Another alternative would be to pay them out of the general cash inflow of funds (premium and interest income) which have always been positive over our data period. This would of course reduce the amount of funds available for reinvestment.

The link between the balance sheet and the revenue statement is through the increase in the life funds which represents an increase in the provision for claims. Table 2.6 gives, in simplified form, two balance sheets for companies. The first is a yearly balance sheet and the other a valuation balance sheet which is drawn up more infrequently

Table 2.7: Cash Flow of the Life Insurance Sector in 1976 (£ million)

Sources of funds	Amount of funds	Percentage of total
Net inflow of funds (sources/uses)[a]	3286	34
Sales etc. of government securities	4565	47
Sales etc. of company securities	1033	11
Sales of other investments[b]	756	8
Total cash flow	9640	100
Net increase (−) in policy loans	−0.6	−
Investable funds	9641	100

a. Excluding policy loans.
b. Excludes cash holdings from previous period.

— for statutory purposes every three years in Britain, though some companies do in fact perform an annual valuation. The object of a balance sheet is of course to compare the liabilities and assets of the fund, and in the yearly balance sheet the investments which back the liabilities can be seen. Whilst this gives a picture of the investments of life offices, it does not indicate any more than that. The investment process of life offices is not to be seen as just a single allocation decision problem. Companies will have securities which are maturing in their portfolios. If they follow an active trading policy this may also provide additional funds. The investment fund manager will thus have funds from two sources: (1) accruing funds from net premium income, net investment income; and (2) funds from the turnover of the existing portfolio (either by maturing assets or conscious decisions to switch). Table 2.7 sets out those linkages for 1976 and we can see that the 'new money' for investment from premium income and investment income makes up 34 per cent of the total cash flow of the life insurance companies. Sales of investments (including maturities) are the dominant item, particularly government securities. These sales can be of securities inherited from a previous period and/or sales of securities purchased in 1976. Sales of company securities only account for 11 per cent of the total cash flow.

Ideally, for our purposes, the valuation of assets in the balance sheet should be at market values. This is only possible in the UK for 1976 (see Tables 2.8 and A.1 (a)). In consequence we have to make do with a mixture of book, nominal and market values.

2.3 Trends in Life Insurance Company Investments

As we have seen earlier, life companies do continue to control large amounts of personal (or household) sector's savings which they invest on their behalf to give the protection and investment attributes of insurance policies written. In Table 2.4 we indicated this link between the sources and uses of funds whilst in Table 2.6 we presented a balance sheet framework of an insurance company. In this section we wish to analyse in some detail the actual balance sheet data for the industry and the net acquisition of assets. The latter is made up of the displacement of new money and the sale of existing assets. This will require us to examine the financial markets within which life companies participate in terms of their relative holdings and share of turnover. This is an essential adjunct in that life companies operate within a financial system and to understand and explain the asset holdings of life companies and their investment policy will require us to know something about the environment within which these investment decisions are made. Table 2.8 gives the percentage of the assets held in each major asset category since 1961 and Table 2.9 gives a maturity split and the percentage each maturity grouping has of the total asset holdings of the portfolio. The data contained in Table 2.8 are not strictly comparable in that the British government securities are valued in nominal terms, whereas the other assets are at book values, except for 1976 where market values are given.[11] It is over this period that the rate of growth of total assets fluctuated quite markedly (see Table 2.10), though the 11.7 per cent rate growth in total assets recorded for 1967 was the result of a revision in the sample. In addition the low figure for 1974 (with the wider coverage) was due to the depreciation of some assets (particularly ordinary shares) in the books of life companies. Overall therefore the total assets of life companies have increased by over 400 per cent, though we might stress that it is important to take account of the changes in the basis of the sample which has increased the coverage of the statistics as illustrated above for 1967 and 1974.

Turning to the constituent parts of the table itself, there are two immediate and striking features. The first is that the portfolio is quite widely diversified. This 'spread' of investments is not prevalent in other countries, particularly the USA (see J.D. Cummins (39)) and it is this diversification we seek to explain in later chapters. The second feature is the apparent great stability in portfolio proportions. Of course by 1961 we would expect that the portfolio imbalance experienced during and after the Second World War would have been removed and this in

Table 2.8: Pattern of Investment of Life Insurance Companies: Percentage of Totals of Holdings of Assets 1961-76 (end year)

Assets	1961	1962	1963	1964	1965	1966	1967[b]	1968	1969	1970	1971	1972	1973[c]	1973[c]	1974[c]	1975	1976	1976[d]
British government and guaranteed securities[a]	25	26	25	25	24	22	24	24	23	22	24	23	23	22	22	26	29	20
UK local authorities	5	5	5	4	4	4	4	3	3	3	2	2	2	2	3	2	2	2
Company securities:																		
Ordinary shares	21	21	21	21	21	20	20	22	22	23	24	26	25	25	21	22	20	28
Unit trust units	–	–	–	–	–	–	–	–	–	–	–	1	1	1	2	2	2	2
Preference shares	5	5	5	4	4	4	3	2	2	1	1	1	1	1	1	1	1	–
Debentures[e]	13	13	14	15	16	18	18	18	17	17	16	15	14	13	12	11	10	7
Mortgages and loans	17	17	17	17	17	18	17	17	17	17	16	15	15	14	14	13	12	12
Land, property and ground rents	10	10	10	10	10	11	11	11	11	12	13	13	14	16	17	19	18	21
Other investments (including overseas government)	2	1	1	1	1	1	1	1	1	1	1	1	1	1	1	–	1	2
Cash and other short-term assets	1	1	1	1	1	1	1	1	1	2	1	2	2	3	6	4	4	4
Agents balance	1	2	1	1	1	2	2	2	2	2	2	2	2	2	2	2	2	2
Total holdings of assets[f]	100	100	100	100	100	100	100	100	100	100	100	100	100	100	100	100	100	100
£ million	6253	6785	7425	8143	8826	9514	10626	11830	12741	13781	15011	16574	18125	19732	20718	23342	25131	24487

a. Nominal values.
b. Includes Commonwealth Life Funds from 1967.
c. Includes an estimate for non-members of the British Insurance Association.
d. Market values except cash and loans and mortgages.
e. We use the terms debentures and corporate bonds interchangeably throughout this study.
f. Rounding error will prevent some of the columns summing to 100 per cent.

Source: Trade and Industry, HMSO

Table 2.9: Life Insurance Companies' Holdings of British Government Securities: Maturities as Percentages of Total Assets 1961-76

Assets and maturity	1961	1962	1963	1964	1965	1966	1967[a]	1968	1969	1970	1971	1972	1973	1973[b]	1974	1975	1976
Up to 5 years	0.1	0.1	0.5	0.5	0.4	0.3	0.9	0.6	0.4	0.3	0.3	0.5	0.5	0.5	0.7	1.7	1.7
Over 5 years up to 10 years	2.3	1.1	1.3	0.9	1.6	0.9	0.9	0.6	0.6	1.0	1.1	1.0	1.6	1.7	1.6	1.3	1.1
Over 10 years up to 15 years	3.9	2.9	2.5	2.1	2.1	2.1	1.8	1.6	1.7	1.3	0.9	0.9	3.2	3.0	2.8	2.3	2.9
Over 15 years	13.7	16.0	15.5	15.7	14.2	13.9	15.8	15.9	16.0	15.3	16.8	16.8	14.3	13.5	14.3	16.4	21.4
Undated	5.5	5.5	5.6	5.4	5.3	5.2	5.0	4.8	4.4	4.3	4.4	3.6	3.3	3.1	2.1	2.3	1.7
Total holdings £ million	1594	1742	1882	2001	2086	2132	2584	2782	2952	3069	3542	3791	4156	4308	4465	5606	7206

a. Includes Commonwealth Life Funds from 1967.
b. Includes an estimate for non-members of the British Insurance Association.

Source: Trade and Industry, HMSO.

Table 2.10: Growth Rates of Total Assets and Net Acquisitions of
Life Companies: 1962-76

	Total assets % growth on the previous year	Net investment in assets % growth on the previous year
1962	8.5	–
1963	9.4	15.8
1964	9.8	7.7
1965	8.4	0.3
1966	7.8	−3.3
1967[a]	11.7	11.6
1968	11.3	−16.0
1969	7.7	−5.1
1970	8.2	11.5
1971	8.9	16.0
1972	10.4	30.1
1973[b]	9.4	4.1
1974[c]	5.0	11.3
1975	12.7	20.1
1976	7.7	18.8

a. From 1967 includes the Commonwealth Life Funds.
b. BIA members only; 19.1 per cent if non-members included for total assets.
c. On a wider coverage to include non-members of the BIA.

part is confirmed by the fact that 1962 was the first year since the
Second World War that British government securities actually increased
their share of the total of the portfolio. Whilst this proportion was
still above that maintained in the 1930s, it was considerably lower than
the post-First World War figures recorded in Table A.3. In fact this
table is quite instructive as it does give the portfolio distributions back
to 1871 for a sample of companies, and even the gap between 1951 and
1961 can be partially filled in by the data published by the Radcliffe
Committee (126) though these data are only for members of the British
Insurance Association so we do not quote them. Indeed overall for the
period from 1871 to the beginning of our data period, there would
appear to have been quite a substantial change in the portfolios of life
companies reflecting perhaps in part changes in investment practice. We
shall be returning to this question in Chapter 3. Initially let us take a
bird's eye view of the trends in the asset distribution for our data period

and then we can concentrate attention on the individual categories of assets later in this section.

Holdings of British government securities have varied within fairly narrow bounds. But if we examine the composition of those holdings in terms of the differing maturities (Table 2.9), we find that longer-term securities dominate the holdings and this has increased over the period (with some variation), though the proportion of undated has been severely reduced over the period. In the medium-term securities, 5 to 15 years to maturity, the overall proportion has dropped but great variation did take place. This overall fall in proportion is broadly matched by an increase in shorts (0 to 5 years) over the period under review.

Although government securities retain a prominent part in the portfolio, holdings of private sector assets (securities, loans and mortgages, land property and ground rents) dominate the portfolio, so that in total they account for 63 per cent in 1976 with public sector securities (British government and local authority securities) accounting for 31 per cent. On market values this increases to 70 per cent and the public sector proportion falls to 22 per cent. The remainder are made up of cash and short-term assets, which were abnormally large in 1973-6, particularly 1976. Other investments (which include overseas government securities) have had a constant 1 per cent since 1962 and agents balances, 2 per cent since 1966. The balance sheet data which make up this table are given in Table A.1 (a) where in addition the loans and mortgages data are further subdivided into house purchase loans, policy loans (since 1971) and other loans.

As we have noted earlier, the proportions are relatively stable, though a few trends are noticeable. Property has seen an overall increase and if we regard this as an equity investment it does not have the same cyclical pattern as the other major equity asset, ordinary shares. But holdings *per se* only give us a static viewpoint of asset displacements and if we examine Table 2.11 we can trace out the net acquisition of the assets in the portfolio (on the same classification as Table 2.8). What this reveals is the variations in the allocation of funds to these assets. In other words, year by year life funds can redirect funds by utilising the new inflow of funds as well as by purchasing and selling securities to arrive at the net acquisition of a particular asset and *in toto*, the net acquisition of all securities. Table 2.11 (with the underlying data given in the appendix Table A.2 (a)) gives a rather different picture of the life companies' portfolio. For a quarterly data series which indicates quite wide variations in net acquisitions as a percentage of the total net acquisitions see Tables A.4 (a) and A.4 (b). Total net acquisitions show a varying growth pattern with 1966 and 1969 recording declines in the absolute cash values of net acquisitions. But of course, these totals will not represent the difference between balance sheet values given in Table A.1 (a) for, as we have noted, the latter are based on a mixture of book values and nominal values, whereas net acquisitions are cash values. If there were an increase in book values of ordinary shares in excess of the net investment for the year, this may reflect the sale during the year of shares standing in the books at the lower prices at which they were purchased in an earlier period. For fixed interest securities this may occur because companies have written down their holdings to take account of a fall in the market price of such assets which accompany a rise in the structure of interest rates. To complicate matters still further (but in the long run improve things) we, of course, also have the market values referred to earlier for 1976.

Taking the private sector securities which dominate the portfolio, then company securities do not appear to take a set proportion of the 'flow of funds'. In some years they have accounted for over 50 per cent yet in other years the proportion has fallen, with the lowest figures accounted by the atypical period 1973/74, with 1974 taking a record low of 4 per cent (if we utilise the unrevised data). The security featuring most instability has been ordinary shares in that over our data period, the range is from 42 per cent (of total net acquisitions) in 1972 to 1 per cent in 1974. Certainly the trend is cyclical, with the amplitude appearing to widen up to 1974, with successive peaks in 1964, 1968, 1972 having successively higher proportions and likewise, at the succeeding troughs, the fall is more considerable. An interesting feature is that net acquisitions of unit trust units (recorded as a separate item only from 1970) held their 1972 proportion in 1974 (and if we take the revised figures sample for 1974 the net acquisition in unit trust units was double that of other types of company securities). This must be partly due to the linking of some policies to the purchase of unit trust units.

Preference shares have declined in significance and as illustrated in Table 2.11 between 1966-72 life companies have been net sellers with no significant acquisition for the period 1972-6. This trend is due to the fall in popularity of preference shares as a means of raising corporate finance with the introduction of Corporation Tax in 1965. This tax innovation gave a dramatic boost to debentures by virtue of the fact that the loan interest could be set against tax as a charge, whereas the

Table 2.11: Life Insurance Companies — Net Investment in Assets — Annual 1962-76

Assets	1962	1963	1964	1965	1966	1967[a]	1968	1969	1970	1971	1972	1973	1974	1974[b]	1975	1976
British government and guaranteed securities	27	19	14	9	4	32	16	16	10	43	20	22	6	8	65	72
UK local authority	3	4	–	4	–	–	2	3	2	1	1	1	2	2	3	2
Company securities:																
Ordinary	15	20	23	11	14	9	24	17	28	30	42	21	1	1	12	10
Unit trust units	–	–	–	–	–	–	–	–	1	1	2	2	2	4	4	4
Preference shares	2	4	2	–	3	6	4	2	2	1	1	–	–	–	–	–
Debentures	19	25	29	33	38	28	27	16	11	11	12	2	1	1	2	4
Mortgages and loans	21	16	20	28	26	13	18	26	14	4	3	19	12	12	3	2
Land, property and ground rents	10	10	9	15	19	15	16	24	24	20	10	22	30	30	21	18
Other investments (including overseas government)	–	–	–	1	1	1	1	1	–	–	–	–	1	1	1	–
Cash and other short-term assets	1	1	3	1	2	4	1	5	13	9	9	10	41	35	14	1
Agents balances	3	2	–	2	4	4	2	2	3	2	3	1	3	5	3	1
Total[c]	100	100	100	100	100	100	100	100	100	100	100	100	100	100	100	100
£ million	506	586	631	633	611	682	791	751	837	971	1270	1322	1323	1472	1768	2101

a. Includes Commonwealth Life Funds from 1967.
b. Includes an estimate for non-members of the British Insurance Association.
c. Rounding error will prevent some of the columns summing to 100 per cent.
Source: Trade and Industry, HMSO.

Table 2.12: Net Investment of Life Insurance Companies in British Government Securities — by Maturity, Cash Values (£ million) 1963-76 as a Percentage of Net Investment of Funds

	Up to 5 years	Over 5 and up to 10 years	Over 10 and up to 15 years	Over 15 years	Undated
1963	3.8	−3.9	3.8	11.3	3.9
1964	−1.1	−2.2	−7.4	23.4	1.9
1965	−2.4	−1.9	5.8	5.5	1.9
1966	−2.0	−10.4	−10.3	25.7	1.6
1967[a]	−7.9	−0.3	2.3	37.8	0.1
1968	−4.4	−1.7	0.7	21.1	0.4
1969	−5.0	−2.8	2.8	20.3	0.6
1970	−1.9	1.4	3.3	5.6	1.9
1971	−0.9	−4.8	1.5	44.3	2.8
1972	2.5	−2.1	−0.5	22.2	−2.1
1973	−2.2	8.7	2.1	13.5	0.3
1974	0.7	1.1	−5.4	11.4	−1.8
1974[b]	0.6	3.6	−5.1	10.4	−1.6
1975	7.8	5.3	−2.9	53.5	1.3
1976	−1.6	1.9	7.0	66.3	−1.7

a. From 1967 includes Commonwealth Life Funds.
b. Including an estimate for non-members of the British Insurance Association.

servicing of preference shares did not receive this concession. In addition, for life offices, franked investment income relief is not important. It is not surprising to see the popularity of debentures as a means of raising finance reflected in the portfolio of life companies and this is certainly the case for 1966 when they formed 38 per cent of total net acquisitions. Thereafter the proportion has declined, particularly for the years 1973 to 1975 and with 1976 actually recording a net sale. These low proportions would appear to reflect the lack of new issues over this period coupled with some redemptions.

Land property and ground rents have a cyclical pattern with the peak occurring in 1974 with 30 per cent of total net acquisitions and with no year falling below 9 per cent. In some imprecise way it would appear that when the proportion of investment in ordinary shares falls, it coincides with an increase in the proportions invested in property and the converse appears to be broadly true. At this stage we cannot be more definite than to offer this observation of the relative cycles.

The last major private sector asset is that of loans and mortgages. In some years the proportion of funds taken up with loans and mortgages has been quite substantial with peaks of 28 per cent in 1965 and 26 per cent in 1966 and 1969. Yet other years, 1971 (4 per cent) and 1972 (3 per cent) the proportion has fallen drastically with 1976 witnessing net sales. The attempt to explain these movements requires a further break-down of the constituent parts of loans and mortgages and this is done, as we have seen, for balance sheet values in Table A.1 (a) and for net acquisition in Table A.2 (a). However, we shall return to analysing this issue in the next section when we conduct a detailed analysis of the purchases and sales as well as net acquisition of all asset types in the portfolio.

Turning to the public sector securities (local authority and British government) these again have shown great variation. In the case of local authority securities, the period 1969-72 saw the net sale of these securities and in other years the proportion does not exceed 4 per cent with this occurring in the early years of our data period. But with British government securities, in some years the proportion has been very high and in others it has been low, with no discernable trend. The period 1962-6 saw a decline from 27 per cent to 4 per cent then a sudden increase in 1967 to 32 per cent, at the time of increasing difficulty with the economy and pressure on the £ sterling (and this increase was at the expense of company securities). The years 1968-70 saw some decline then a sudden increase in 1971, apparently at the expense of mortgages and loans and short-term assets to give 43 per cent share of net inflow. 1972 saw the proportion fall to 20 per cent and in 1974 it fell to 6 per cent. But 1974 was an atypical year in that cash and short-term assets had 41 per cent of the inflow reflecting the uncertainty that life companies (and other investors) had in financial markets. This was repeated in 1970 when the previous peak for short-term assets was 13 per cent and British government securities took only 10 per cent of the total allocation of funds. Yet in the following year there was a run down in these short-term assets, as we have seen, which coincided with a record net acquisition of British government securities. The situation for 1975 and 1976 is largely the same except that both had massive net acquisitions with gilts taking 72 per cent of total net acquisitions in 1976. These large net purchases were again at the expense of liquid assets, mortgages and loans.

In these tables we are not distinguishing differing maturities within this asset type, although it is possible to break the maturity range down to five classifications; 0—5 years, 5—10 years, 10—15 years, over 15 years and undated. This we do in Table 2.9 and Table 2.12. As we would expect, the longer term securities are more significant in the portfolio with 21 per cent in 1976 for the over-15 year securities, though the undated have shown an overall decline in their share over the period to 1.7 per cent. The short securities (0—5), although still small (less than 2 per cent), have nevertheless increased their share whilst the medium-term securities, 5—15 years, have shown a mixed performance with some years accounting for under 2 per cent (1972). With the net investment the position is even more dramatic. The over-15 year securities have had a positive net investment on an annual basis for the period 1962-76, but the proportion has varied from 66 per cent in 1976 to just over 5 per cent in 1965 and 1970. The cyclical activity broadly matches that for all British government securities noted in Table 2.11 apart from the years 1964 and 1966 which gave two successive peaks to the over-15 year securities and troughs to the total. But whilst the broad cycles may coincide, the total net acquisitions over our data period reveal (see Tables A.2 (a) and A.2 (b) for the actual data) that for eight years (1964, 1966-9, 1971-2 and 1974) the net acquisitions of longs (5—15 years) exceeds the total net acquisition of gilts, reflecting the net sale of other maturities. These sales have been predominantly of shorts and mediums, though the undated had net sales in 1972 and 1974. If we take the shorts (0—5 years) there were only three years out of thirteen when there were positive net acquisitions and whilst the overall proportion of shorts has increased in terms of holdings, this is likely to have been achieved through the passage of time, as long and medium securities held in the portfolio range become progressively shorter in terms. In medium-term securities (5—15 years) there were four years when life companies were net acquirers with some years when the net acquisition of the two market segments within this group (5—10 and 10—15 years) behaved in a similar fashion; with other years when the movements were in the opposite direction: for instance in 1963, net sales of 5—10 years and net purchases of 10—15 years maturities.

The last major group of assets held by life assurance companies are short-term assets. These are made up of cash in hand and with UK banks, UK local authority bills and temporary money and other. We have already indicated that these would appear to be abnormally large in some years, particularly in 1973 and 1974. It would appear therefore that there are periods when life companies would seem quite willing to build up their short-term assets and then subsequently run them down, so that the holdings might be beyond those which are necessary for the transactions purpose of life business. The widening cycles noted in holdings are also reflected in the net acquisitions, which in Table 2.11, on an annual basis, show successive peaks of 3 per cent, 4 per cent, 13 per cent and 41 per cent in the years 1964, 1967, 1970 and 1974, respectively.

2.4 Characteristics of the Eligible Set (for Life Companies) of Financial Assets

In the preceding section we have analysed the holdings and net acquisitions of life offices for the period 1963-76. We have observed the apparent wide diversification of asset types and in this section we need to examine the essential characteristics of the assets which life offices do hold.

Financial assets do differ quite markedly with respect to coupon, maturity dates, marketability, default risk, income and capital risk and transaction costs and therefore merely to compare the observed yields (even where this is possible), will not necessarily provide much of a guide when comparing assets with a view to holding them in the portfolio. In addition, the impact of inflation will not be felt equally across the returns from the securities held. However, whilst some of these assets may be substitutes for one another, others may be complements and as a necessary first step we need to examine these relationships. We can attempt this by examining the attributes of each of the main asset classes. We commence with government marketable securities which offer many advantages to investors. J.B. Marshall (103) gives a very good discussion of the various characteristics and attributes of government securities. They are default free, they give security of income, they have supreme marketability at low cost and in large blocks and, subject to a minimum holding period of one year, they are not taxable on realised gains (since 1969). In addition they are available in a variety of maturity dates and coupons. The government security market is a focal point of participation by life companies as well as being (as we shall see in Chapter 3), a standard of comparison with other types of assets. Decisions in this market affect other markets because rates on gilts are the lynch pin of other rates. But whilst gilts have this advantage, they also have two disadvantages, namely that their market value can vary and their real value falls with inflation. Whilst there are capital gains to be made from gilts, as the recent fall (1977) in interest rates reveals, over the longer period market losses can be made and inflation eats into the real return.[12]

Corporate bonds have some similarities to gilts in that they are usually redeemable (but often shorter than many of the long government bonds) and they generally have a fixed coupon and *a priori* claim on the assets of the firm. This imparts a strong element of capital safety, though the yield will or should cover an element of risk premium to cater for the possibility of default. In fact corporate bonds are distinguished in terms of yield by their credit standing. In that sense they are comparable with government bonds, but their marketability differs. In the first instance they will only normally be purchased as 'new issues' and whilst there is a secondary market in them, it is much thinner (as we shall see in Section 2.5) so that active buying and selling of existing issues can cause more movement in prices than the same volume traded in gilts. Market yield is therefore not necessarily independent of the activities of life companies given the position they hold in this market and in consequence opportunities for switching profits are limited.

One of the biggest drawbacks to corporate bonds is the availability of stock. The extent to which demand can be satisfied given the propensity to acquire new issues is limited by the overall supply and this itself will be a reflection of the environment within which business operates. Business profits reflecting the ability to service the fixed charge that corporate debt brings do fluctuate quite markedly, so that at times there are a dearth of issues and other times a flood of them. In consequence there is often a bunching of stocks with similar coupons (no lower coupons for net funds) and maturity dates and as time passes (and given that the length of life at issue is generally shorter than similar government issues), then insurance companies can find themselves cluttered with a mass of short-dated stock which they may have difficulty selling to move longer.

We have already said that the quality of the stock[13] should be reflected in the yield and there would be a powerful argument advanced for life companies to go for quality (given their aim of security) and to leave the lower quality issues at a discount for other investors. However, there would appear to be a considerable variance of views among life companies on this question and the only published evidence is for the USA. W.B. Hickman (82) found, for example, that lower quality issues carried higher default risk but provided higher promised and realised yields suggestive therefore of opportunities for investment.

The other corporate fixed interest security available is that of preference shares, but as we have already indicated, they have declined in importance as taxation changes have rendered their issue *vis-à-vis* debentures an expensive method of raising capital. Their supply is therefore very limited and the market is small and one-way. They are normally irredeemable and are often subject to call options (often exercised when interest rates are low). In consequence their market price can fluctuate quite widely. In addition as there is no absolute security of income or security against inflation there has to be a substantial margin in yield over debentures and gilts to cover all these disadvantages.

Life offices have changed their investment strategy (see A.C. Murray (111) for example) since the nineteenth century and in fact then it was the mortgage markets which constituted the major asset of life offices (a dominance which is still evident in the USA with 34 per cent of their total assets in 1974 in mortgages). This concentration then in Britain was quite understandable from both the point of view of what the mortgages offer the investment manager, as well as the fact that it was not until the 1850s that stock exchange securities were available in sufficient quantities as investment media, particularly in the corporate sector. What mortgages do not possess is liquidity, in that there is no secondary market in them. But they can satisfy two of the other criteria reviewed earlier, in that they are longer term (but domestic mortgages can often only average 7-8 years, see page 30) and normally have abundant security, given a realistic valuation of the property and the normal lending rules. In addition they give a measure of diversification to the portfolio. To compensate for their lack of marketability they should carry a yield above that of corporate bonds. This is not always possible because in the house purchase market at least, life insurance companies will have to compete with building societies. In fact, they do not attempt to compete actively, rather they use the house purchase market as a vehicle for obtaining new life business, so that overall the yield is often secondary and unattractive. But house mortgages were about 50 per cent (in 1976) of the total mortgages and loans with the remainder going to industry and commercial borrowers. Whilst mortgages can have advantages in terms of their maturity, there are still disadvantages. They are liable to one way call features on the part of the borrower and they are costly in terms of resources to select and set up and there can be a lag before they are taken up. If they are carefully selected they tend to be trouble free, but as with other fixed interest securities, they are not covered for inflation.

Fixed interest securities, gilts, corporate bonds, mortgages and loans and to a smaller extent preference shares, do have an important role to play in the portfolio of life companies. Their particular attributes make them ideal investments which can be shaped to cover the liabilities and, in some instances, the particular tax position of some funds. Thus those life offices with a high proportion of non-profit insurance and immediate annuities we would expect to have a higher proportion of fixed interest. R.L. Carter and J.E.V. Johnson (27) cite an instance of one life office with nearly 95 per cent of its invested funds in holdings of mortgages and loans by virtue of it having originated as a building society. In consequence most of its current life securities are linked to the provision of domestic mortgages.

With fixed interest dated securities there are two questions: (1) what is the yield to maturity;[14] and (2) how certain are the fixed coupon payments? But with equity investment a further question needs to be posed: (3) how large are future earnings expected to be and, following on from this, what are other people's expectations of these earnings? By equity investment we mean principally ordinary shares and to a lesser extent holdings of property and both these we regard as substitutes for one another and as possible substitutes and complements to the fixed interest assets discussed so far. If we take ordinary shares first, because they carry no prior claim on the assets of the company they are the risk bearing element of the capital structure of firms. To evaluate shares (for a discussion of methods of review see D. Weaver and B.G.H. Fowler (166)) it is necessary to take cognisance of the overall political and economic trends, as well as how well individual firms are managed and their profit records over time. This does require a sizeable investment in resources and to justify it there must be a commitment to a significant investment in ordinary shares. For a general coverage of equity investment and life funds in the UK see P.E. Moody (109). The holdings have to be reviewed continually too, but our argument throughout this study is that this should apply to all holdings, not just to equity. This, as we shall see in the next chapter, is not a view shared by all investment managers. Company profits are a residual and a fluctuating proportion of GDP and, of course, equity earnings are themselves a residual of company profits, so this factor makes them cyclical and less certain. It is for this reason that they have been viewed (and still are) with some suspicion. Yet as we shall indicate in Chapter 3, there were moves in the early twentieth century actively to encourage investment in ordinary shares which (see Table A.3) only accounted for 2 per cent of life offices portfolios in 1915, though a steady rise can be discerned after 1930. This is not surprising, as increasingly, ordinary shares came to be viewed more favourably as actuaries felt that standards of financial practice in companies had improved. Even at the present time (1979) there is some residual suspicion and certainly quite different views are held by life investment managers. This is also true, perhaps more so, with property investment.

The gradual move to equity investment can be illustrated by the following quotation:

> It would be interesting and valuable if we could ascertain or estimate with any degree of accuracy what would be the effect of investing ... in what may be called speculative investment ... I by no means advocate a trial experiment in practice but it might be useful if anybody possessed of the necessary patience and perseverance would make the experiment on paper by selecting a number of such securities and following their fortunes to see what the result would be (President of the Institute of Actuaries, 1903).

In addition, various commentators gave specific illustrations of how ordinary shares had 'outshone' debentures and how they were able to insulate against the effect of inflation. One of these early studies for the UK was by H.E. Raynes (127) (128): at the time of writing (1927) only 4.3 per cent of life offices' portfolios were in ordinary shares, but one office he reports did have 16 per cent. His work was intended to encourage life companies to hold ordinary shares in that his investigation showed that for the sample chosen, companies need not depart from well established criteria of security of capital and adequacy of investment return to achieve better results in terms of yield.[15] What the study revealed was that for supply and yield 'a well-spread investment in ordinary shares is a better proposition for the ordinary long-term investor than an investment in the debenture issues of the same group of companies' ((127), p. 29). Indeed not only were the dividends higher than the interest received on bonds over this period, but the market value of shares showed a capital growth, whereas the bonds showed a loss of market value, assuming a sale prior to maturity. So on the question of currency depreciation, ordinary shares well compensated for this over the period. This particular investigation is illustrative of the questions which were being raised, not necessarily over relegating safety of capital to a secondary role, but about how this safety could best be achieved: this is evident even in the wider literature of the period as T.S. Eliot wrote — 'Everything is in question, even the fundamental dogma of modern society that debentures are safer than common stocks.'

H.E. Raynes also did a follow-up study in 1937 (128). He recognised that the depression years may have distorted the situation. Using a larger group of companies[16] he found a further capital growth in shares but the prices on fixed interest securities also revived considerably. The return in the form of income however, showed little difference between the two groups.

Ordinary shares have no maturity date so that by holding equities it means that life funds cannot match the duration of assets to liabilities. Because they are irredeemable, they do, as we shall see in Chapter 3, have a place in a fund, particularly with regard to a policy of 'immunisation' against the effects of interest rate changes. However, holdings are fully consistent with another aspect of their liabilities in that they can give the protection against inflation; though a long view is necessary. At times the market can fall dramatically as was witnessed in the UK between 1974/5[17] and this can cause the same 'locking in' which can occur in fixed interest stock when interest rates rise. Nevertheless it would appear that over the long term, ordinary shares can give protection against a modest inflation rate and provide a hedge against rising interest rates. The market is active with financial institutions forming over 50 per cent of the volume and trading so it would appear that there are gains to be made, in both the short and long run. The handling of an equity share portfolio clearly requires personal judgement to take advantage of perceived gains; though some purchases are made by taking up the rights issues on existing holdings. But even here the investment manager will still have the choice to take up the 'rights' or to sell them in the market.

Investment in property *per se* (rather than the shares of property companies or the holdings of ground rents) has been a post-war trend (see E.K. Read (132) for a discussion of life offices property investment), and it is not surprising that as property represents a large proportion of the nation's wealth, that financial institutions should regard it as an asset for their portfolios. Not only is it a long-term investment which can yield income in the form of rents, but there are capital gains to be made from the increasing valuation of the property. However, there is no formalised secondary market in property and it has been subject to external interferences via legislation, taxes, rent controls, etc. Nevertheless by virtue of it offering a hedge against inflation, it has its attractions and of course it is possible to diversify holdings of premises by type of holding (offices, houses/flats) and by geographical placings. In fact life offices in Britain have been active property developers, often in partnership with local councils or other developers which stands in contrast to the position prior to the Second World War when, apart from their own properties, some of which they let off, investment in property was limited to freehold ground rents.

So our review of the characteristics and attributes of the various financial assets leads us to summarise possible *a priori* hypotheses with respect to complementarity and substitutability which we detail in Table 2.13. (See S. Royama and K. Hamada (143) for a detailed discussion of substitution and complementarity in the choices of risky assets.) Fixed interest securities of mortgages and loans, corporate bonds and government securities we detail as being substitutes for one another and complements to ordinary shares and property investment which both offer a hedge against moderate inflation and, though their marketability is rather different, we still regard the two as substitutes.

Table 2.13: Hypotheses of Asset Substitution and Complementarity

Asset pairs		A priori hypotheses
Ordinary shares	— property[a]	substitutes
Ordinary shares	— corporate bonds	complements
Ordinary shares	— government bonds	complements
Ordinary shares	— mortgages and loans	complements
Corporate bonds	— government bonds	substitutes
Corporate bonds	— mortgages and loans	substitutes
Government bonds	— property	complements

a. Direct investment and ground rents.

The other remaining type of investment (which is clearly residual in both the balance sheet and in net acquisitions) is that of overseas investment. In this study we will not estimate equations to explain holdings (or changes) of these assets but it is worth while analysing some of the considerations which affect their purchase. It is to be expected that life companies should purchase overseas assets, particularly from those funds which arise locally (e.g. in the case of Commonwealth Life Funds) and indeed it is necessary, as L.C. Polke and G.J. Titford (124) have argued for the distinction to be made between using UK originated funds and those that have arisen locally. In the case of the latter, the normal principle of matching can be applicable in that a liability in one currency should be matched or covered by assets expressed in that same currency, though this might not always be possible given the availability of assets in these countries. However, it would appear that at times, life offices have given increasing attention to the possibility of using UK funds in search of higher returns, particularly with integration into Europe and the differing economic experience of other industrial countries compared to Britain. It is of course possible to invest indirectly overseas so as to benefit from the expansion (or otherwise overseas) by investing in UK companies with significant overseas interests. But this does not of itself remove the exchange rate risk problem. This movement of funds is still very marginal as is evidenced by the balance sheet data (which reveal that overseas government hold a dominant but decreasing relative share to overseas loans and mortgages). In fact, they account for under 10 per cent of the total assets. The net investment on an annual basis is given in Table A.2 (a). Even accepting the smallness of the sums involved, however, this type of investment is likely to grow as it can both increase the overall return on the portfolio and give further room to manoeuvre. But if they are being purchased with UK funds, the return must be significantly better than that available in the UK, or there must be some other compelling reason to invest (e.g. prospects for further life and other insurance business). The problems of investing overseas are well-documented elsewhere (see for example L.C. Polke and G.J. Titford (124)), but suffice it to say here that this is an area which in future is likely to see an expansion of interest; particularly in assets where it is possible to assess their risk—return attributes.

2.5 The Role of Life Companies in Financial Markets

So far we have examined the portfolio and net investment of life companies in a vacuum as it were and the purpose of this section is to place life companies in perspective in terms of the financial markets within which they operate. This it is hoped will then enable us to understand their investment policy and the effects this may have on these markets. But one aspect of our discussions in this section is the question of how important life companies are in the markets in which they invest. This can be summarised in terms of their 'dominance' in those markets. Having said that, we need to establish some criteria for this. By dominance we mean that the actions of investors, in our case life companies, will be transmitted to the market in terms of price so that the price and yield established in the market will not be independent of their actions. But do we measure dominance in respect of holdings, trading and/or net acquisitions? Holdings *per se* are unlikely to give this effect period by period so that it is more likely to be trading and the overall net acquisitions which can move the market. Thus one can conceive of a market where one class of investor is dominant in terms of holdings but another investor, say with only 10 per cent of total holdings, can, via its trading, be effectively dominant in terms of price and even the terms on which securities are offered for sale as new issues (with respect to say coupon, maturity, etc.). In consequence in analysing the role life companies play in financial markets it will be necessary to analyse this from these three viewpoints: (1) holdings; (2) trading (purchases and sales) including activity or turnover rates; and (3) net acquisitions. Table 2.14 gives the life insurance companies' holdings of marketable securities expressed as a percentage of total market holdings for four years within our data period. What this reveals for government securities is that they do hold a significant share of the longer (i.e. over 5 years) bonds. This is a rather restrictive maturity split but the only one possible as data on total market holdings is only available on this basis. If we had included the data on the other participants in the market, we would have found that in 1976, the next major holder of the over 5 years stocks were the pension funds with a 14 per cent share. In fixed interest securities, particularly debentures, life companies are unquestionably the dominant holder and the concentration in the market is reinforced by the fact that in 1976 pension funds also had a 30 per cent share. In other words there are few other participants in the market. For ordinary shares their share is relatively low but they are the second largest holder among the financial institutions who in 1976 held over 40 per cent of the total market holdings. So overall, the share held by life offices of these important markets has increased over the reference period.

Table 2.14: Life Insurance Companies' Holdings of Marketable Securities as a Percentage of Total Market Holdings (31 March) 1964-76

Securities	Government securities[a]		Fixed interest company securities[b]		Ordinary shares[b]
Year (31 March)	Total	Over 5 years	Preference shares	Debentures	
	%	%	%	%	%
1964	13	18	25	43	7
1970	19	26	30	34	10
1974	20	26	37	65	15
1976	20	31	30	63	12

a. Nominal values.
b. Book values.
Source: Financial Statistics, HMSO.

To obtain a better picture of the activities of life offices in these markets we need to examine purchases and sales both in terms of the market in toto (Table 2.15), and in terms of relationships of life office purchases to sales and sales to total portfolio holdings. An examination of Table 2.15 illustrates that whereas in 1964, life offices dominated both the purchases and sales undertaken by financial institutions, this share has fallen by 1976 to just over one-third of the total government securities market. This experience of a fall in shares is broadly found in the other markets of company fixed interest and ordinary shares.

Table 2.15: Life Insurance Companies' Purchases and Sales as a Percentage of the Total Undertaken by Financial Institutions (Excluding Banks)

| Securities | Government securities | | Fixed interest | | | | Ordinary shares | |
| | | | Preference shares | | Debentures | | | |
Years	P	S	P	S	P	S	P	S
1964	62.71	59.94	50.00	40.00	67.56	53.01	23.73	19.70
1970	40.01	41.51	12.50	34.48	44.21	41.21	22.21	16.77
1974	55.21	56.06	21.43	20.97	49.07	42.95	21.87	19.48
1976	38.26	36.28	26.50	34.85	35.52	47.80	15.53	15.49

Source: Financial Statistics, HMSO.

Another dimension to obtain some other measure of market activity is to use turnover ratios. (For a similar approach see R.L. Carter and J.E.V. Johnson (27).) These give an estimate of the extent to which life offices turn over their portfolio of assets. Various rates can be used and we specify below the use of two such ratios.

(1) *Ratio I*

$$\frac{\Sigma S}{\Sigma P}$$

where ΣS = total sales in the period of each asset class at market (cash) prices.
ΣP = total purchases in the period of each asset class at market (cash) prices.

(2)   *Ratio II*

$$\frac{\Sigma S}{\overline{TH}}$$

where

$$\overline{TH} = \frac{TH_t + TH_{t-1}}{2}$$

and TH_t = total holdings of each type of asset at book nominal or market values.[19]

We present in Table 2.16 the activity ratios for five markets; government bonds, debentures, ordinary shares,[20] property and loans and mortgages. The first three securities possess recognised secondary markets whereas the other two do not. One or two interesting features emerge from these. In the first instance for most years and securities, purchases and sales (ratio I) are broadly related though this is less apparent for property. The strongest relationship is to be found in government securities, which is what we would expect in terms of their marketability. But even in debentures where the market is regarded as relatively thin, and in loans and mortgages where there is no ready market, purchases and sales are quite strongly related. One interesting trend reported on by S. Mason (105) is that some financial institutions are reducing the number of holdings of shares thereby reducing diversification to concentrate holdings in the larger companies so as to enable greater marketability.

The more interesting ratio is that which gives an idea of the turnover of the whole portfolio holdings of the asset (ratio II). The supreme marketability of gilts allowed the life office in 1974, for example, to turn over its whole government bonds portfolio by 80 per cent. Whilst all the other securities have featured an increase in this other turnover measure, sales as a proportion of average total holdings as given in ratio II are relatively low.

The final dimension by which we can assess life offices *vis-à-vis* other market participants is in their final net acquisitions. Of course this is just a netting out of the purchases and sales but we do quote the data for the same years utilised in the other tables. These data are given in Tables 2.17 and 2.18. For government securities of over 5 years to maturity life insurance companies are confirmed as the major net acquirer and this is repeated for debentures, apart from 1976 when they were net sellers. In ordinary shares pension funds dominate out life companies and in 1976 this was to the extent of five to one.

Table 2.16: Turnover Ratios[a] of Financial Securities by Life Insurance Companies 1964-76

Securities	British government securities		Debentures		Ordinary shares		Property		Loans and mortgages	
Years	I	II	I	II	I	II	I	II	I	II
1964	0.87	0.31	0.19	0.04	0.39	0.06	0.17	0.02	0.52	0.09
1970	0.94	0.42	0.61	0.06	0.55	0.10	0.13	0.19	0.64	0.09
1974	0.97	0.80	0.91	0.07	0.97	0.14	0.42	0.06	0.62	0.09
1976	0.75	0.71	1.45	0.11	0.78	0.14	0.48	0.06	1.09	0.14
1976[b]		(0.75)		(0.13)		(0.12)		(0.06)		—

a. Where I = $\Sigma S/\Sigma P$; II = $\Sigma S/\overline{TH}$.
Where ΣS is total sales in each period; ΣP is total purchases in each period; $\overline{TH}$ is average holdings (for the calculation see p. 69).
b. Market values.

Table 2.17: Net Acquisitions of British Government Securities — £ million — Analysis by Financial Institution, 1964-76

Institution	Deposit banks		Building societies		Pension funds	Unit and investment trusts		Life insurance companies	
Years	0–5	Over 5 years	0–5	Over 5 years	All securities	0–5	Over 5 years	0–5	Over 5 years
1964	−68	−111		4	6		−16	− 7	99
1970	169	− 37	114	101	−21	−18	4	−16	100
1974	48	1	14	47	88	28	14	9	107[a]
1976	NA[b]	NA	67	105	1171	− 4	10	−34	1547

a. Includes the estimate for non-members of the British Insurance Association.
b. Data are now available only for stocks up to 1 year and over 1 year.

Source: Financial Statistics, HMSO.

Table 2.18: Net Acquisitions of UK Company Securities — £ million — Analysis by Financial Institution, 1964-76

Securities £m	Debentures			Ordinary shares		
Years	Life insurance companies	Pension funds	Unit and investment trusts	Life offices	Pension funds	Unit and investment trusts
1964	184	60	5	142	220	67
1970	89	79	−6	232	391	20
1974	16	−27	−13	13	254	−106
1976	−87	9	17	201	1115	34

Source: Financial Statistics, HMSO.

Table 2.19: Life Insurance Companies' Holdings and Net Acquisitions of Loans and Mortgages — Annual: 1961-76 (£ million)

	Holdings				Net acquisitions		
	House purchase loans	Other loans and mortgages[c]			House purchase loans	Other loans and mortgages[c]	
1961	634	388		1961	NA	NA	
1962	685	450		1962	NA	NA	
1963	719	508		1963	32	59	
1964	768	587		1964	49	78	
1965	848	677		1965	87	91	
1966	876	820		1966	63	96	
1967	909	905		1967	33	57	
1968	1021	986		1968	69	74	
1969	1080	1102		1969	80	108	
1970	1117	1186		1970	34	78	
1971	1132	1248	(194)[a]	1971	11	30	(0.2)[a]
1972	1110	1283	(188)	1972	−21	46	(−0.1)
1973	1218	1425	(194)	1973	109	139	(7.0)
1973[b]	1229	1456	(204)	1974	105	53	(16.0)
1974	1381	1556	(293)	1974[b]	107	63	(20.0)
1975	1439	1558	(264)	1975	58	−3	(4.5)
1976	1447	1510	(263)	1976	8	−52	(−0.6)

a. Policy loans.
b. Includes estimates for non-members of the BIA.
c. Excluding loans overseas.
NA — not available.

Source: Financial Statistics, HMSO.

The other two major private sector assets in the portfolio of life companies are 'land property and ground rents' and 'loans and mortgages'. Neither of these two types of assets have a ready secondary market and both broad groupings do not fully reflect the diversity of asset types within them. For instance the holding of ground rents (fixed income) is a rather different asset to say office and commercial property let out for rent, or agricultural land. Unfortunately it is not possible to disaggregate this grouping though it is possible to do it for loans and mortgages.

If we analyse the 'property' asset first we recall that we discussed the broad pattern of this grouping in relation to the whole portfolio, both in terms of its balance sheet significance and in terms of the net acquisition of assets period by period. We noted (Table 2.8) that there had been an overall increase in holdings from 10 per cent to 19 per cent over the reference period with the main increase being evident from 1970. Yearly fluctuations however, appeared quite significant with the range being 9 per cent in 1964 and 30 per cent in 1974 of net acquisitions (Table 2.11) and if we were to examine the quarterly data on net acquisitions (Table A.4 (a)) the fluctuations are even more acute with the range being 2 per cent to 40 per cent of total net acquisitions.

Of course investment in property *per se* (as opposed to say the acquisition of ground rents) can be a fairly 'lumpy' process in that the acquisition of office blocks and such like can involve quite large sums in a given period. But equally life companies have been active in 'on-going' developments in partnership with others (including local authorities) which would involve more regular sums to be required as the development project progresses. Without any firm evidence, it is difficult to give a definitive judgement on this heterogeneous item and as to how the various assets within it determine the final outcome of the data. What we can witness is an increasing interest in the overall 'property' class by life companies, and also by superannuation funds. So whilst life companies have shown a great awareness of investment in this asset class, so has another long-term investor. An examination of the two turnover ratios indicate that sales turnover within a given year can be quite high (for later years) with respect to purchases but low in terms of the whole portfolio of property held. On the margin they appear to be willing and able to sell some of the property assets, but some of these sales may not be conscious decisions to sell since some leaseholders may well be exercising their rights to purchase the lease.

Turning to the data on loans and mortgages, included in this grouping are loans and mortgages to commercial undertakings, property developers, policy loans and a small amount to overseas borrowers. It is not possible to be very specific about this rather amorphous grouping, although it is possible to break the data series down into house purchase loans, other loans and mortgages and, since 1971, policy loans — and this we do in Table 2.19. If we analyse the data in this table we see that in terms of 'holdings' up to 1968, house purchase loans are the largest item within this grouping. Yet after this period, other loans and mortgages (which includes policy loans, which were identified separately from 1971) became the dominant asset type. On the net acquisitions, apart from 1974-6, house purchase loans do not have a major share of

Table 2.20: Loans for House Purchase by Financial Institutions – Annual 1963-76 – £ million

	Advances				Repayment of principal				Net advances				
	Total	Building societies	Local authorities	Insurance companies	Total	Building societies	Local authorities	Insurance companies	Total	Building societies	Local authorities	Insurance companies	Others
1964	1380	1052	196	132	659	505	75	79	753	546	121	53	33
1970	2355	2021	180	154	1159	933	108	118	1246	1088	72	36	50
1974	3828	2950	629	249	1753	1460	164	129	2278	1490	465	120	203
1976	6568	6117	249	202	2907	3499	219	189	3836	3618	30	13	175

Source: Financial Statistics, HMSO.

funds flowing into this type of asset but in fact in 1972, there was an actual decline. On the turnover of loans and mortgages, on ratio I this is quite high due partly to the repayment of mortgages (see Table 2.20), but on ratio II the turnover is low. If we can concentrate attention on the 'house loan' market, as a market, Table 2.20 indicates that the role of insurance companies and life insurance companies in particular is limited and even with a book value of housing mortgages of £1447m in 1976, it is still only a mere 6 per cent of building society mortgages for the same period.

2.6 Conclusion

We now wish to draw the various threads together of the description and analysis of the flow of funds through life insurance companies because the data presented in this chapter constitute the basis of this study. Therefore we can offer now a check list of the main points which we have raised in this chapter.

1. Whilst life companies have experienced considerable overall growth in the source of funds, this growth has been volatile and when account is taken of the various uses to which these funds are put — claims on policies, management expenses and taxation — the amount which represents the saving of the policy-holders, the provision for future claims is not as predictable as one would have expected *a priori*.

2. These provisions for future claims represent the liabilities of the life companies and the policies written by the companies will be of different types requiring rather different provisions by the investment officers. Annuities, for instance, require the company to pay a fixed sum each year until the death, whereas with endowment with-profits, the payment is made only on death or maturity. What we illustrated was that in the calculation of premiums, an assumed rate of interest is used with assumed rates of mortality, management expenses and the like. Many policies are long term over which these conditions may vary and of particular significance is the rate of return written into policies which is effectively the cost of capital to companies. What we did illustrate was that a cushion is provided by bonus loading on with-profit policies. Nevertheless, there is a commitment there (apart from linked policies) to earn a particular rate of interest and this commitment can extend over a very long period. In this sense, the insurance contract is perhaps unique in terms of offering such a 'fixed' term commitment unlike many other forms of investment. Though, as we have argued in Chapter 1, the balances held in insurance contracts are

unlikely to be regarded in the same way as deposits in building societies, banks or other financial institutions.

3. It is the provision for future claims and the turnover in the existing portfolio that gives the investment managers the funds to invest in the various financial investments available. The striking feature of this investment of funds is that the portfolios of companies are very diversified. They extend into virtually all financial markets as well as property and other 'real' or capital assets. We noted that in terms of holdings (recognising the valuation problems already discussed) the proportions appeared to be relatively stable over a period when assets increased by over 400 per cent. An increasing trend in short-term assets was, however, noted particularly in the last few years of the period.

4. Although this stability was noted in the proportions of holdings it was not confirmed when account was taken of the 'net acquisitions' (in cash values) of the various assets. An examination of the proportions that the various assets have of net acquisitions on a quarterly basis is given in Tables A.4 (a) and A.4 (b). It would appear from these data that life companies can redirect funds quite quickly and there were periods when they were net sellers of particular securities.

5. The overall emphasis of the portfolio and net acquisitions to it is based on longer-term assets; but that is not to say that shorter-term assets are not purchased (e.g. short government bonds) over and above those held for liquidity reasons (reasons which may include the holding of a mobile reserve for longer-term investment). Additionally long-term assets may be sold, perhaps after a relatively short holding period. This is evidenced in the relatively large element of trading (ratio I $\Sigma S/\Sigma P$) in many markets, even for assets in which there is no recognised secondary market, e.g. property. Trading activity is particularly significant in the equity and government securities markets where transactions are often very large in a given quarter, yet the net result, i.e. net acquisitions, may be quite small. However, turnover as measured by ratio II indicated that sales as a proportion of total holdings can be large for government securities, emphasising their supreme marketability, but relatively low for the other assets.

6. Given the holdings, net acquisitions and trading that life companies have, their position in financial markets must be evaluated as this may give them a degree of power in markets such that they become dominant. We examined some of the criteria which could be used to indicate dominance and which could possibly lead to the actions of life offices turning prices against themselves in the market. This might well be the case for the fixed interest security market, particularly

for debentures; but a significant proportion of purchases are made from new issues, so that this may well reduce the effects of being a large holder and trader. Life offices are also the most important single investor in the 'long' end of the government securities market, but this does not of itself imply that they are a 'dominant' investor in terms of the criteria of dominance adopted. This is especially so given that there are other institutional investors active in this part of the market. Turning to the market for ordinary shares, whilst life offices are still a significant force in the market, it would appear that they could not be termed the dominant investor.

Notes

1. A level premium is charged for an increasing risk: for an enlarged discussion and illumination of the principles underlying level premiums see G. Clayton and W.T. Osborn (33) and J.R.S. Revell (135).

2. These illustrations are given for closed funds and drawn using data supplied by B.H. Davies.

3. In practice life offices use different rates for assurances, for general annuity business and for pension annuity business, therefore it is no longer appropriate to think of a single rate for valuation purposes. What they do is to use recent gilt edged redemption yields making some provision in the case of long-term policies at annual premiums for a future reduction in interest rates. Judgement will clearly be used to avoid getting too much out of line with the market at any point. Certainly life officers like to watch their competitive position as regards premium rates and they tend to be forward looking such that there may be a feedback from this competitiveness to investment policy. In this regard we are referring to the movement, particularly since the Second World War, into equity assets and also the greater emphasis now given to market trading of assets.

4. The method of valuing liabilities creates a 'new business strain', i.e. the actuarial reserve exceeds the addition to the fund in the first year. Thus an over-rapid expansion of new business would cut into surplus available for distribution and would cause a subsequent slow-down. The capital needs for expansion are such that only a controlled, internally financed expansion is possible.

5. For a discussion of the question of solvency see H. Ammeter (2) and R.S. Skerman (153). For a coverage of solvency see G.E. Pinches and J.S. Treischmann (123) and for solvency and regulation as it applies to banks see J.R.S. Revell (136). J.L. Anderson and J.D. Binns (3) give a useful overview of actuarial management.

6. In general the financial problems are similar whether the life office is mutual or proprietory or composite. In the case of mutual companies the policy-holders own the company and are entitled to all the profits whereas in other offices the particular constitution of the office will determine the share. In practice the distinction from the point of view of the policy-holder is small. But in neither case are non-profit policy-holders given a bonus to reflect the higher interest rates earned on contracts taken out when premiums were based on lower rates of interest.

7. Apart from a single premium policy this is not realistic but it simplifies the analysis. The block of policies, in this case *i*, are homogeneous with respect to type, age of policy-holder, length of policy, etc.

8. It was from the Dalton era that the ideas for matching and immunisation developed. For a modern treatment see A.D. Sheddon (147).

9. It would be feasible to conduct life assurance without interest income and holding investment as 'cash' but it would be a costly procedure to policy-holders.

10. In the past policy loans were often given on advantageous terms to the borrower but now a market rate is charged. The problem of policy loans, however, is far less acute in Britain than in the USA.

11. These market value data do reveal that fixed interest securities are standing at lower values than their book values (in the case of debentures, preference shares) and nominal values (in the case of government securities).

12. See A.J. Merrett and A. Sykes (107) for the real returns 1919-61, de Zoete and Bevan (44) for 1919-72 and I.G. Richardson (137) (138) for an analysis which extends back to 1960 for Consols, 1900 for short-dated gilt-edged stock and 1930 for equity. S. Wynn (169) gives a useful discussion of real rates of return for the UK and other countries. Other studies include N. Barr (7) and S. Bird (12).

13. There are no standard or established methods of grading industrial debentures and loan stocks compared to the USA where Moody's and Standard and Poor's rating have been widely used for 50 years and more. However, this situation is under review in the UK. See British Bond Ratings (20) an exposure draft produced by a joint study group of the Institute of Actuaries and the Society of Investment Analysts and also see 'British Bond Ratings – A Reply' (21), a document prepared for the Accepting Houses Committee and the Executive Committee of the Issuing Houses Association.

14. In the case of mortgages and loans with fixed par values the yield to maturity is equivalent to the coupon payments.

15. To be specific he took a sample of 54 companies in nine industrial groups (the six largest in each group) for a 15-year period (31 March 1912 to 31 March 1927). An initial investment was presumed to have been made of £54,000 (£1,000 in each company) in a portfolio of ordinary shares and £54,000 in a portfolio of fixed interest (for the same companies) including redeemable and irredeemable. The yield on ordinary shares was always in excess of 5 per cent net upon the original investment and for the fixed interest under 3 per cent for four successive years. The yield gap started at 1½ per cent spread to 3.3 per cent in 1919 and remained at over 3 per cent thereafter. No intelligent switching was allowed so better results could have been obtained by selling out some shares (which had persistently declined, e.g. railways) and reinvesting elsewhere. The capital growth of the shares was to £80,073, whereas the bonds showed a loss of market value to £42,583 assuming a sale prior to maturity.

16. This revised sample contained the original 54 companies. The market value of ordinary shares at the height of the depression at the end of 1931 was 118.6 per cent of their purchase price in 1912 and for fixed interest it was 76.42 per cent. He then constructed a new series for the period 1 January 1927 to 31 December 1936. Eleven industrial groupings were used in 66 companies. The original investment of £66,000 grew to £97,144 in the case of ordinary shares and £89,400 for fixed interest. The income return was £34,880 for shares and £34,423 for bonds.

17. For a discussion of variability of returns on ordinary shares in the USA see L. Fisher and J.H. Lorie (57).

18. There is also the question of 'dominance' within the sector itself. This is a problem that we recognise but we cannot handle in this study. Certainly the Prudential Insurance Company by virtue of its 'size' does reportedly find its investment activities constrained.

19. In the event we only have market values for 1976, as has been discussed

already.

20. Sales will be liquidations not always initiated by the life office itself, for instance liquidations of house mortgages.

3 THE OBJECTIVES AND CONSTRAINTS ON INVESTMENT POLICY

3.1 Introduction

We have seen that life offices provide two functions. In the first place they provide cover against the risk of death or of survival and secondly they act as investment managers by providing a guarantee of income, in the case of annuities, and a guarantee of future capital security and of long-term investment yield in the case of insurance and assurance policies.

Our analysis of the sources and uses of funds, the portfolio dispositions of life companies and their trading in financial markets leads us to pose the following two questions which will occupy our attention for this and subsequent chapters of this study:

1. What factors underlie and constrain investment managers?
2. What objective(s) can we ascribe to them?

The format we adopt in this chapter is to attempt to answer these questions *seriatim*.

3.2 Factors Underlying and Constraining Investment Policy

Whilst life offices have considerable freedom in their investment decisions, their actions are still bounded. Although they can and do influence and shape the environment within which they operate, they cannot determine it. We can recognise two groups of factors which affect and mould the investment decisions of the life offices, *external* and *internal* influences. We can at this stage list the subdivisions under these two broad headings and then cover them *seriatim*.

External	(i)	government regulation
	(ii)	taxation
	(iii)	exchange rate risks and regulations
	(iv)	supply and market constraints
	(v)	inflation
Internal	(i)	nature of the liabilities written
	(ii)	capital risk
	(iii)	income risk

(iv)   liquidity considerations
(v)   administrative and organisational limits

External

(i) Governments have solvency and regulatory powers over financial institutions and these have been particularly important in the case of banks, because of their role in the payment mechanism and in their ability to create 'money'. But life offices (and general funds) are also subjected to government control, though these controls in Britain are relatively recent and are not as specific as those in the USA and most other developed countries. The need for some regulation and control comes from the fact that as life offices provide a primary source of protection and an important medium of saving, they should not be allowed to default in their policies[1] as not only would this cause hardship to the community as a whole, but it could threaten the structure of the whole financial system. We have already discussed in Chapter 1 the extent of this control and whilst it certainly conditions life office investment within the overall limits set on the investment in particular securities (and controls in the case of new offices up to a five-year period), these are unlikely ever to act as an 'effective' constraint on investment. However, it is felt that there will be a progressive tightening. Where the controls do have an effect is on the proposed solvency valuation conditions, which are on break-up values and more particularly the valuation of the liabilities. Rules for valuation of assets are in force with some assets being inadmissable for solvency purposes. On the valuation of liabilities the position is more fluid. Here the DTI proposed in their much criticised draft regulations (which are not in line with EEC standards) no more than 90 per cent of the current yield being earned by the company. In consequence the particular regulation can have a potent effect on investment behaviour. This can be illustrated by reference to fixed interest securities. If a reverse yield gap exists between dividend yields on ordinary shares and redemption yields on government securities, then this would appear to favour the acquisition of British government securities (with the added feature of tax advantages on realised gains that we cover later in this section). Additionally another feature has been a widening of the difference between redemption yields on long and short bonds so this gives an added dimension to the issue. However, the emergence of a reverse yield gap can be linked to inflationary expectations and we cover this issue in the fourth external constraint.

(ii) Taxation has an important part to play in conditioning investment policy. In the first instance the fact that life policies (as we saw in Chapter 1) carry a 'tax subsidy' encourages the whole medium of life assurance and at various times, certain tax advantages have prompted the growth of particular types of policies which have rather different characteristics to other policies, perhaps requiring a different emphasis on investment policy. More significantly with regard to investments is the tax treatment of the funds themselves, as the income which they generate from the assets, as we have seen, is quite substantial and this is made up of dividends and other interest payments and realised net gains. G.M. Dickinson (45) has made the point that as life offices are concerned with their post-tax returns, then the inter-relationship of their own corporate tax position and that of the assets in the eligible set is an important consideration. Capital gains on gilts in the assurance fund we know are free of gains tax if held for one year or more but this applies to any investor. The preference for 'low coupon' short stocks favoured by some investors (high marginal rate income tax payers) does not apply to institutions such as life offices. Perhaps of more significance is the fact that the annuity business side of the office is treated differently. If the general annuity fund is paying out more immediate annuities than it is receiving in investment income the income is free of tax, but the fund would be taxed on profit not reserved for policy-holders.

(iii) Life offices do (as noted in Chapter 2) derive premium income from overseas and the contract will be expressed in the currency of the country of origin. In fact, as we have seen, the UK authorities maintain the stance that domestic liabilities should be backed by assets held in the UK. If subsequently the £ was devalued against this currency *vis-à-vis* there could be a loss, unless the office invested in currency assets of the country of origin so as broadly to eliminate the currency risk. In fact many overseas countries have minimum deposit requirements which have the effect of removing such a risk.

(iv) Whilst life offices may have the desire to pursue a particular type of investment policy, whether it be to buy for example debentures or to sell some of the existing portfolio, their ability to do so will be conditioned by the market. There may be supply constraints which limit the availability of a particular security in the quantities they require with the right features (e.g. maturity coupon, etc.). Additionally, life offices may be prevented from selling, either by the lack of suitable secondary markets and/or by market imperfections which limit or effectively prevent the sale of the stock. This is an important issue that will be referred to later in this chapter and in

Chapter 4. The supply constraint is not so relevant in the gilt-edged market, where there is some evidence of tailoring the debt.

(v) Whilst the normal life contract (as opposed to the unit-linked business of life offices) is expressed in nominal terms so that companies can provide for their *contractual* obligation, there is perhaps an implicit contract that in the case of savings biased policies the real value of capital will be maintained; though many life managers would not agree directly with this. What they would say is that in an inflationary world dividend and rental growth will more than make up for the reverse yield gap in the long run. We shall return to this point later in this section but we can argue at this juncture that concern with 'inflation' can provide an important conditioner to the choice of investments. We can illustrate this by reference to the emergence (after 1960), of the reverse yield gap. To some commentators (see for example J.L. Carr (24)) the existence of a reverse yield gap signifies that investors feel that they have less to lose from holding ordinary shares (in terms of movements in profits and falling stock market values) than the risk (via falling real values) of holding fixed interest securities. The fact that equities can on the whole give some long-term protection against inflation *vis-à-vis* fixed interest, we demonstrated in Chapter 2. But this fact probably penetrated to the majority of investors over our data period, so that the observed 'yield gap' can itself be the result of such views with a shift away from fixed interest into equities, particularly with substitution occurring at the long end of the gilt-edged market. However, the experience of the 1973-4 falling stock market values has re-emphasised the volatility of shares. In addition, dividend controls and the failure of some quite large companies has produced the need for more caution in the evaluation of long-term prospects.

Internal

(i) We have in Chapter 1 already discussed the types of policies (and their magnitude) which life offices issue. All these policies offer a guarantee which requires different investment provisions to be made. For instance the payments guaranteed in an annuity contract require a company to provide a specified outgo over a long period. In consequence the investment of funds must take account of the liabilities (given the actuarial assumptions of mortality) and what that requires, income, capital sum and so on. In consequence the financial structure of a life office must not just be seen as a portfolio of assets to meet contractual liabilities, but an inter-relationship of the cash flow of assets and liabilities. In fulfilling these contractual obligations the life office faces particular risks and we cover these in (ii) and (iii) below.

(ii) Capital risk (security) can have at least two aspects, (a) default when payment is due and (b) variations in the market values of the security due to interest rate changes and other considerations affecting the price of the asset. Default risk, as we have seen, is not a factor with British government securities but is present to a greater or lesser extent in all other assets. Liquid assets do not suffer from fluctuations in market value, but there is risk of default depending on the status of the debtor. Loans and mortgages are also fixed in nominal terms, but are of course subject to default risk. In order to be competitive most offices seek the higher returns which go with the riskier long-term assets suitable to match their abilities and are able to face up to both elements of capital risk. In fact an examination of the portfolio of life offices reveals (see Chapter 2) that in 1976 over 80 per cent of the total assets is accounted for by assets which do not give capital security, and if we were to exclude 'real' assets giving some protection for inflation, we would find that in 1976 over 60 per cent of the portfolio was in assets which over the longer period would not offer much insulation against inflation. It would appear that whilst companies must clearly evaluate default risk (e.g. going for quality) and attempt to take account of changing capital values caused by interest rate movements and events in the economy, overall it would not appear to restrict the type of investment. This stands in contrast to the views held prior to the Second World War which were based primarily on A.H. Bailey's canons (5) the first principle of which was 'the security of the capital'. For a discussion of Bailey's canons, particularly in a modern-day context see J.C. Dodds (48).

(iii) We can interpret income risk as arising from two sources: income default and investment of future premium, though this interpretation does not find universal agreement. Taking the former, income from investments may be variable, as is the case in ordinary shares. But there can also be income default from so-called fixed-income securities as there is always a proportion of mortgages and house purchase loans in default. Some offices, for instance, have moved into the higher-risk second mortgage business where income default is common, often leading to capital default. In the case of future premiums, apart from single premium policies and immediate annuities, life offices receive premiums over the life of the particular policy and also accruing interest payments and maturing or realised assets have to be reinvested. Given that life offices have written a guarantee in the contract, then this future investment has to be made at unknown future rates of interest, and in the Dalton era of cheap money there was the fear that life offices might not be able to earn the rate of interest assumed in their policies. It was to combat this that the matching and immunisation policies were developed, though the origins of such approaches are to be seen in pre-Second World War writings — see for example R.R. Tilt (161), R.J. Kirton (92), D.C.H. Potter (125), A.T. Haynes (74), A.T. Haynes and R.J. Kirton (75). Insulation against such declines in interest rates could be achieved by investing the assets so that they match the estimated liabilities both by amount and date. This form of matching can be referred to as *absolute* matching and this is to be found in the writings of D.J. Robertson and I.L.B. Sturrock (140) and A.T. Haynes and R.J. Kirton (76). The constraints on such a policy in terms of the availability of stock as well as the difficulty of matching a growing fund are in part taken account of in the F.M. Redington (133) policy of *immunisation* which involves the life office in matching the mean term of its liabilities with the mean term of its assets. For a stationary fund (new business just equalling maturing policies) the logic of the immunisation approach would be to have a steady process of selling shorts and buying longs to maintain the same mean term. With a growing fund this involves the life office in a policy of going over long.

As the majority of life policies are long term, then it is not surprising to see the concentration of the portfolio of assets that we saw in Chapter 2 focusing on the longer term including irredeemable. Concern for income security may be to the detriment of policy-holders, particularly the with-profit, as a policy of immunisation is against profit as it is against loss. In consequence it may inhibit manoeuvrability and lead to failure to exploit movements in markets. Additionally life offices are insulated against a fall in income by virtue of the income reserve that we referred to in Chapter 2.

(iv) In studying some of the other financial institutions in Britain such as banks and building societies we can observe that there are 'statutory' liquidity requirements. In the banks, these are referred to as reserve requirements and the eligible assets that can enter this classification are quite tightly specified. In the case of building societies the 7½ per cent liquidity ratio refers to all assets other than mortgages and there are various other ways in which building societies determine their own operational liquidity ratio, which is in the main in excess of the 'statutory' one (see G. Clayton, J.C. Dodds, M.J. Driscoll and J.L. Ford (32)). In turning to life offices we find that there is no externally imposed liquidity requirement so that holdings of liquid assets are, or would appear to be, a choice asset. We know also from our discussions in Chapter 2 that most life offices generate a substantial net inflow of funds (there are some closed funds in existence) and apart from the needs for administrative costs, surrenders and policy loans there is a positive net flow available for investment. This cushion of free income coupled with the cushions available from the 'hidden' reserves is available if there were to be any sudden cash drain or if the fund were to be subjected to a catastrophic decline in the value of the underlying assets. Clearly, as we have argued in our discussion of the capital risk of life companies, at any given time life offices may hold securities which have market values below acquisition costs. But as life offices can take the long view, this need not be an important consideration, provided the future investment income is not likely to be seriously affected. If excess short-term assets (over and above those required for the normal transactions such as settling claims, etc.) are essentially a choice asset, then they may represent a temporary abode of investment until the new funds are invested more permanently and/or they may represent liquidations from other assets previously held. Together they can give a fund an ability to manoeuvre and they may indeed be regarded as part of the free reserves (or estate or solvency margin) of the offices which are available to support investment policy — an issue we shall return to later in Chapter 5. In fact, if assets are regarded as segmented between free reserves and liabilities, liquid assets would probably be matched against short term liabilities rather than against free reserves although they would nevertheless provide flexibility in varying investment policy.

(v) Unless the investment policy is in some way predetermined, which could arise if there was a well-developed forward commitment process as in the USA (see J.J. O'Leary (114)), then investment managers have to possess information on securities with respect to their capital and income attributes. If they buy to hold, then only the initial evaluation is necessary, unless they wish to measure portfolio performance so as to provide a progress report. But if, as we have seen, they wish to trade in financial markets for one reason or another, then they require more information, particularly in the way of forecasts and facilities to appraise the existing portfolio, as well as merely the disposal of new funds and funds from maturing assets. For a coverage of information flows available see S. Mason (104). Such information goes beyond merely measuring performance and requires analysis of the portfolio performance and estimation of future cash flows and degrees of risk. This point is developed by P.O. Dietz (46).

Some offices, as we have indicated, specialise more in one type of security than others so their portfolio needs will differ. But overall we can argue that search costs will be high if a more active investment policy is called for, but the rewards are there in terms of assisting management with improving performance. In consequence, what is required is an ability to measure the performance of various classes of securities in the portfolio and thus measure the effectiveness of the investment decisions made by the portfolio managers, with a view to improving future decisions.

3.3 The Objectives of Life Offices

So far we have reviewed the factors that appear to underlie the life insurance industry in terms of the liabilities they issue, the constraints on their behaviour, the assets they hold and we have seen in Chapter 2 that their portfolios cover a very wide spectrum of assets. The funds they invest (from the new inflow) and reinvest (from maturities and sales) are enormous and represent a pressure on investment managers to seek new outlets and where possible to utilise fully the existing markets. We are thus disposed to ask the question: why is it that they adopt a particular investment pattern?

Traditional economic theory stresses the purposeful behaviour of individuals and institutions so this implies that economic agents must have objective(s) to which action is then directed. If we borrow from the neo-classical theory of the firm, the motivation is maximisation of profit. This unitary objective has been criticised both from the point of view that with the presence of uncertainty, maximisation of profit is a meaningless phrase and from the point of view that firms, even if they could maximise profits, do not wish to. Instead they have other objectives which reflect the organisational elements within the firm, particularly the managerial interests. Whilst life offices are rather different to the firms of manufacturing industry and the like, there are many similarities, and in fact the latter are in our view more important than the more obvious differences of service *vis-à-vis* the manufacture of capital and consumer goods. We can list these similarities:

1. They are organisational entities.
2. There is separation of management and control. Indeed, this is taken to the extreme in the mutual offices where there are no shareholders as such and the with-profits policy-holders own the office.

In consequence there is no check provided by shareholders, but the policy-holders have the right to attend Annual General Meetings and elect Directors in much the same way as do shareholders in a proprietary company.

3. They are perpetual entities. Although the life insurance contract is time dated, the offices are continually writing new business so that they are open funds.

But can we be more specific about objectives? We can recognise from the above that firms have a dominant aim of survival[2] and this can be achieved if they remain solvent. This is seen to be particularly important in the interest of the policy-holders and the community as a whole as well as to the management of the office. It has now become unacceptable for life offices to default on their policies because they offer a primary source of protection as well as an important medium of saving. A. de Morgan (43) writing in 1838 argued that 'it may be said there is nothing in the Commercial World which approaches even remotely the security of a well-established and prudently managed insurance office'. This viewpoint has received some 'shocks' in recent years with the failure of a few life offices. These failures have, however, reinforced the desire of the established offices to demonstrate their ultimate safety. A mass default would throw the whole financial system into turmoil. In consequence, life offices often regard themselves in a quasi-trustee role. Quasi because whilst the relationship between life offices and policy-holders is one of retailer and consumer, insurance policies and annuities are in essence contracts, and in consequence the relationship between the management and the policy-holders takes the form of a trustee and beneficiary (as vested in the directors). Life offices need to earn a target rate of profit (that is guaranteed) to avoid the disaster of insolvency. But such a viewpoint implies a static view of investment policy and of the liabilities which are issued. Indeed, the target rate of return specified is likely to exceed the minimum which must be earned, and this mark-up margin, if we can think of it in these terms, may vary over time and among life offices. See Chapter 2, pp. 41-3, for a more specific coverage.

As well as being concerned with survival through time it is likely that companies will be concerned with 'growth' of total life business (premium income or sums assured) and the corollary, total assets. Whilst this objective is more difficult[3] to substantiate on the part of life managers, the growth objective is commonly referred to in industrial firms (see for example J. Bridge and J.C. Dodds (18) for a coverage of the growth objective in firms) and in financial institutions – see for example G. Clayton *et al.* (32) for a discussion of the objectives of building societies. Companies to grow through time[4] need, by virtue of the problem of time gearing to diversify the products they offer as consumer preferences change. We have noted in Chapter 2 how, even over the relatively short span of years of our own data period, some changes have occurred in policies issued, which therefore produce a structural change in liabilities. Growth may also be linked to managerial objectives in that we can recognise that managerial objectives may be quite a significant force, particularly in mutual offices where there are not the checks that the 'market' and to a lesser extent the shareholders can give to proprietary offices. (An additional factor according to F.M. Redington (133) and G.V. Bayley and W. Perks (9) is to preserve a reasonable equity between classes and generations of policy-holders.) Growth can also bring with it status and security to managers, but the growth objective as a *managerial objective* need not of itself imply that this is to the detriment of profit. Indeed R.L. Marris (102) illustrated that under certain assumptions the two need not conflict. However, the bulk of literature available on the organisational and behavioural revisions to the theory of the firm point more to satisficing behaviour as regards profit (or rate of return) which is linked to an aspiration level. This level is not just determined by the industry itself but will be influenced by competition from the savings media. Indeed outside pressures may cause a continual revision in this aspiration level. Perhaps the greatest force for revision will be the competitive pressures from within the industry, either from new entrants and/or from an evaluation of the performance of different offices. On this latter point it is quite significant that the rates of return achieved by different offices do vary quite markedly for the same class of business.[5] Whilst this may be seen as a spur to some life offices to do better, the fact that these differences often do persist, may also point to the fact that they are not an effective motivator.

If these corporate control mechanisms are sufficiently strong in their operation, we would then appear to have a growth and profit objective reconciled in some way. The ability to achieve any of these objectives will however be conditioned and constrained by the factors discussed earlier. If the objectives are to be expressed in terms of growth and profit, then this implies something further about the nature of life offices; they must plan. Planning comes from the need to diversify the product line and the need to appraise the alternative investment outlets, not only for the new funds but also for the existing funds tied up in particular assets. The move for example that life offices have made into equity investment since the Second World War is to be seen as a step towards diversifying the asset mix, as well as taking account of the need to seek higher returns. This step could not have been taken (and maintained) without the necessary appraisal. If therefore life offices are to be continually appraising their assets and liabilities, this implies quite heavy search costs to provide the information with which to monitor and control these decisions. But these decisions are undertaken in an uncertain world so that investment managers have to take a view as to future conditions. They might not have to worry unduly about the liabilities side as they do have the large contractual element, but in their investment policy they are brought face to face with uncertainty. Uncertainty which will affect their judgements as to the 'default' risk of securities and more particularly to the likely movements in the structure of interest rates; movements which can bring quite substantial gains or losses to underlying securities. In these circumstances we must preface growth and profit by the word 'expected' and indeed if we appraise the actuarial literature on life office objectives we find reference to this issue of expected profit. In 1948, J.B.H. Pegler (119) argued that the main principle of investment should be the expected yield and H.G. Clarke (28) in 1954 put the objective as being 'to maximise the expected yield with the minimum of error, having regard to the nature and incidence of the liabilities'. Subsequently J.G. Day (40) argued that the availability of reserves would limit the degree of risk a life office could afford. The G. Clayton and W.T. Osborn (33) study also argued that this was the objective and G.T. Pepper (120) likewise stressed expected yield to be the fundamental principle of investment. He goes on to argue that this principle should be applied, not only to the selection of individual stocks, but in terms of the analysis of the portfolio as a whole. In other words, not only should investment managers compare the relative expected yields on the available investment opportunities as they allocate their inflow of funds, but they should also review their whole portfolio with a view to making changes in its distribution. In contrast, E.H. Lever (96) illustrated that one view held prior to the Second World War and, perhaps since, was that gilt-edged securities could be locked up and forgotten about, until the annual audit. But what do we mean by expected yield? We can define it in terms of the holding period of the asset and, if this is known, the expected yield is calculated by taking the coupon or dividend payments due, if any (in the case of say ordinary shares, the expected dividend), together with the estimate of the probability of the return of the capital and the receipt of the income. The expected yield can then be calculated as a return on the acquisition price of the asset. The expected yield, therefore, is different to the 'apparent yield' at the time of acquisition, which for ordinary shares could be the dividend yield (based on the dividend paid in the last financial year) or the earnings yield. As we do not know *a priori* what the holding period is, some assessment has to be made so as to provide information for the monitoring and control procedure discussed already. A common viewpoint, no doubt influenced by balance sheet consideration, points to a one-year assessment. This is to be found in the literature appertaining both to the UK and the USA — see for example B.G. Malkiel (100) for the USA. Pepper for instance calculated one-year yields for the gilt market made up of interest plus the capital gain/loss. Similarly S. Benjamin (11) used one year returns as a measure of gain and J.R. Hemsted (79) (p. 20) extended the concept of one year returns to 'not only provide some measure of overall efficiency in the use of limited resources but . . . also [to] provide a means of assessing the degree of overall risk to the life office'.

It is of course possible to reconcile the 'expected' and 'apparent' yield if we can argue that investment managers have static expectations of the Hicksian (83) type such that they expect the apparent yields in $t + 1$, and certainly the viewpoint is suggested by both H.G. Clarke (28) and H.C. Cottrell (37) who argue that it is the apparent yield used in the assessment of a security of the apparent yield gap when comparing different asset classes. Of course investors can be wrong in their forecast or assessment as the events unfold themselves so that the actual or realised yield is an *ex post* yield which is derived at the time of sale or maturity. But it is only of relevance in comparison to the expected yield if the actual holding period were to be the same as the assessment in the calculation of the expected yield. However, the literature is full of more complicated procedures to generate expected yields or utilise proxies[6] for them, and the present writer has made extensive use of these in the past. We use the word generate[7] wisely because as D. Meiselman (106) for one has observed (in connection with the bond market) 'Independent evidence of interest rate expectation is virtually unobtainable and behaviour based on those expectations is revealed only by the phenomena we seek to explain' (p. 18).

In essence three hypotheses have been used in the literature though within each different variants have been adopted. All are mechanistic in their use of past yield data with the *extrapolative* hypothesising[8] that the market will be influenced by the most recent changes in the rate of interest in forming its future expectations of that rate. Thus if expectations are elastic, then if there have been recent increases in this rate, for example, the long-term rate, the investors may expect the rate to continue to rise. The converse argument would hold too. With increasing rates then the expectation would be for capital losses and with falling rates, capital gains. This hypothesis of Duesenberry (52) thus relates the expected capital gains/losses to the difference between the actual long-term rate and immediately past long-term rates. There are alternatives open to us but the emphasis must be on relatively recent past rates in the weighting scheme used. Various lag schemes are available taking different periods and different weights. We could for instance weight the past values equally so that if we take two such values R^L_{t-1} and R^L_{t-2} the weights of 0.5 are applied to each and the results summed to produce the expected rate (R^L_e) in t. If we change the weight pattern and adopt what is nearly an Almon (1) lag then we could weight the most recent, $t-1$ more heavily – say 0.75 – and the $t-2$ with the difference, in this case 0.25. Another scheme which is worthy of note is to take the rate in $t-1$ and add to it the difference between the rates in the previous two periods:

$$R^L_{et} = R^L_{t-1} + \left(\frac{R^L_{t-2} - R^L_{t-3}}{2} \right) \tag{3.1}$$

Certainly extrapolative schemes are used extensively in the literature and the error learning and adaptive expectations mechanisms of D. Meiselman (106), P. Cagan (23) and R.M. Solow (156) as used not only in the formulation of expected interest rates but also inflation are a special case of the extrapolative mechanisms.

An alternative schema is a *regressive* one which embodies the Keynesian concept (91) of the normal rate or range of interest rates which found further support in J. Robinson (141) and B.G. Malkiel (100). It is against this backcloth that investors judge the likely changes in specific interest rates; changes which will determine the capital gains and losses to be expected. This normal rate is a long term rate and if the current (or spot) rate is above this normal rate, capital gains are to be expected because interest rates will fall and vice-versa – this expectation appears to be based on a City of London proverb: 'What goes up must come down.' It is difficult to determine these normal rates and the normal range within which interest rates will move, but *the* rate and/or the upper and lower levels of the range are normally calculated by using a distributed lag or moving average formulation of previous rates. Whilst the normal rate or range of interest rates is an interesting development, we are still left with the task of determining what this rate will be. One method used in the literature (see for example J.C. Dodds and J.L. Ford (51), is the Koyck lag (94) where the normal rate is represented as a geometrically declining weighted average of past (actual values) of the long-term rate of interest back to $t - n + 1$. Equation (3.2) illustrates the use of the Koyck transformation

$$L_t^N = \sum_{i=0}^{n} \lambda^{i+1} L_t - (i+1) \quad 0 < \lambda < 1 \tag{3.2}$$

and in Equation (3.3), the sum of the weights, λ^{i+1}, equals unity irrespective of the value of λ.

$$L_t^N = \sum_{i=0}^{n} (1-\lambda)\lambda^i L_t - (i+1) \quad 0 < \lambda < 1 \tag{3.3}$$

The Koyck transformation frees us from the need to compute a normal series *per se* but the next step is to utilise the proxied normal series to assess the investors' expectations of gains and losses from changes in interest rates. This can be achieved by approximating these by the difference between the actual long rate and this 'normal' rate. We can represent this (in linearised form) as Equation (3.4), namely

$$NA_t = a + b(L - L^N)t \tag{3.4}$$

where NA_t is the net acquisition of the particular asset
        L the actual long rate
        L^N the calculated normal rate.

But to argue that expectations are either extrapolative or regressive is to dichotomise the process. These two views are not necessarily divergent and de Leeuw (42) in his pioneering work on the financial sector of the USA married these two hypotheses together. This approach was following a suggestion by J. Duesenberry (52) and the de Leeuw hypothesis was subsequently adopted by F. Modigliani and R.S. Sutch (108). He calculated, prior to estimation, values of the normal rate utilising a particular form of a distributed lag function (an inverted V). The weights here could be varied such that they produced

Keynesian (long-lags) and Duesenberry (short-lags) variables. The de Leeuw representation of this mixture of regressive and extrapolative mechanisms is contained in equation (3.5) which is taken, with a minor change in notation, from his financial model.

$$R_e^G (\lambda) = R_t^G - (\frac{1 - \lambda}{1 - \lambda^{11}} \sum_{i=1}^{11} \lambda^{i=1} R_t^G - i) \qquad (3.5)$$

where $R_e^G(\lambda)$ is the capital gain/loss on government securities and R_t^G is the yield in period t and where λ was allowed to vary from 0.15, 0.25, . . . up to 0.95. As de Leeuw indicates, with λ set to 0.15, this is virtually a first difference and with $\lambda = 0.95$ it 'is the current value in relation to a much longer average' (p. 500).

The normal rate is given by the second term on the RHS of the equation and the presumption that de Leeuw advanced was that the coefficient of this second term should be opposite in sign to the coefficient of the first one. Whilst these three schemes do produce expected series, we feel that the Hicksian caveat that in reality investors will be unlikely to have 'precise expectations' is a useful reminder that we are dealing with a difficult concept to model. If this is linked to the Clarke and Cottrell argument developed earlier that current yields may be taken as a guide to the near term future, then perhaps we have justification for the use of static expectations.

We have argued that life offices may wish to review their existing portfolio as well as to place the new funds accruing. In consequence we need to examine the balance sheets of offices as well as the net addition to these. Our discussions about the purposeful growth and profit objectives of life offices and the need for planning would suggest that a life office should have some desired structure both in terms of its product-mix (liabilities) and the assets it has to meet these, and the incidence of these period by period. This desired balance sheet structure need not be directly observable and generally the portfolio will not be in equilibrium, so that as new funds are available for investment they can be used to reduce the gap between the perceived optimum ratios and the actual proportions. Some evidence on the use of proportions is to be found in J.R.S. Revell (135). At the extreme, allocation could be done in terms of fixed proportions characterised as a fixed coefficient input—output model. It is unlikely to be of this type, but for a treatment of a flow of funds input—output model in the case of building societies see G. Clayton, J.C. Dodds, M.J. Driscoll and J.L. Ford (32). Additionally they may also shuffle their existing assets (within market

constraints) to bring about the desired changes in the portfolio allocation, though this adjustment will of course reflect the cost of adjustment,
e.g. transactions costs and the degree of adjustment required.

We are therefore arguing, following H.I. Ansoff (4), that the investment decision can be split into a hierarchy of *strategic* decisions which
reflect the overall balance of investment, i.e. decisions between
different classes of security (allocation and switching decision between
classes) and operational or tactical decisions which reflect lower order
decisions to allocate and switch *within* particular classes. In this process
mean variance (E.V.) analysis (as developed by H. Markowitz (101) and
others) may be used. It can only be used in the strategic choice under
very restrictive assumptions. To be able to select the optimal fractions
of total wealth each class of, say, bonds and equity should have, we
must know the proportions of all equities in the equity part of the portfolio and likewise for bonds. If, however, there is only one equity asset
and one bond then we can solve for the two optimal holdings. This
study is focusing on the strategic decisions, though *en passant* we have
noted the trading within security classes. The third type of decision
Ansoff recognises is that of the administrative ones, those which
provide the information flow and the machinery to effect the operational and strategic. This would involve a process of investment or
security analysis and would involve not just stock exchange securities
but property, mortgages and other assets. To achieve this requires an
analysis of indicators in the economy and, in the case of company
securities, an analysis of industries and individual firms.

But given the objectives already specified and the constraints which
may shape the decisions can we posit a review mechanism? We would
argue that such a mechanism would be contained within the administrative framework so as to provide the two levels of decision-making
with the necessary appraisal. The objective of the portfolio performance measurement would then be to test the effectiveness of the
investment decision, given the objectives set, with a view to improving
further performance.

We are therefore implying regular, if not continual, supervision and,
as we have already indicated, this requires a comprehensive mass of
information from a variety of sources, as well as an analysis of these
data. What would be continually under review would be the principal
division between fixed interest and equities (including property), as
such a division would appear to be a major matter of policy and hence
is to be regarded as a strategic decision. Of course, as we have argued
previously, within each security group there will be opportunities for

operational switching and this is particularly true of gilts. But even for ordinary shares, an examination of share indices illustrates substantial variation in the returns offered by different securities. In consequence, the performance process needs to be both dynamic and adaptive. Having said that, we are still left with the difficulty of specifying the mechanics of this performance process.[9] From our discussions with investment managers of life offices, it would appear that continual measurement of performance of the fund is secondary to the investment of the future cash inflow. This, however, is less true of the managed funds and unit-linked funds where, by virtue of the daily publication of bond and unit values, more emphasis is given, to performance, if only for comparative purposes. Investment managers do, however, undertake periodic reviews particularly as regards to the strategic mix of fixed interest and equity assets and this will be prompted by changing market conditions, the inflow of funds and the type of policies written — for instance more with-profits business given its longer term may lessen the pressure on life offices. Our argument is that this performance appraisal ought to be on a more continuous basis. In consequence we need to concentrate attention on 'stock' and 'flow' considerations, and perhaps place primary emphasis on flow influences[10] as well as recognising that disequilibrium in holdings can exist. We are therefore brought face to face with the need to specify a dynamic framework and this can be done by utilising the standard partial stock adjustment mechanism as illustrated in Equation (3.6) as used to model the life assurance sector by T.M. Ryan (144) for the UK (see Chapter 4) and J.D. Cummins (39) for the USA.

$$A^a_t = A^a_{t-1} + \alpha(A^*_t - A^a_{t-1}) \quad 0 < \alpha < 1 \tag{3.6}$$

where A^a represents the actual demand for asset A; and
         A^* is the desired or optimum holding of that asset.

If we were to take A^a_{t-1} to the left hand side of Equation (3.6), we would have an expression explaining the change in the holding of asset A, period by period. Several forms of this simple dynamic adjustment mechanism are possible and one that is often employed is that a constant proportion of the difference between the desired and actual holdings of the particular asset is reduced in the period following a change in the explanatory variables, say interest rate structure. This adjustment is often portrayed by means of a lagged dependent variable. Adjustment can be brought about by a redirection of the inflowing funds and the net acquisitions data illustrate[11] that at times companies can virtually ignore a particular market, yet at other times place a substantial amount of funds into it, and this trend would appear to be increasing. Additionally, they appear to be willing to build up short-term assets which they can then run down when they perceive profitable avenues for investment. They appear to wish to remain fully invested, to be earning a return on their funds, but they give themselves room to manoeuvre in times of uncertainty in some financial markets by going 'short'. This of course may involve them in some risk in that rates may move against them, but what they may be doing is trading off interest rate security for capital security.

We now wish to formalise the ideas we have presented above and set out in Equation (3.7) what the typical function may look like

$$NA_i = a_{io} + \sum_{j=1}^{n} a_{ij} R_j + \sum_{k=1}^{m} b_{ik} S_k \tag{3.7}$$

In this equation we are stating that the net acquisitions[12] of the ith asset (NA_i) are a linear[13] function of a vector of yield returns $R_1, \ldots, R_n$ and a vector of other explanatory variables and/or constraints $S_c, \ldots, S_m$.[14] What these contain would depend on the focus of the model in terms of emphasis on stock or flow elements. As we have already indicated, a stock adjustment model could include a lagged dependent variable. A pure 'flow' model would have an income constraint in the form of net new money for investment. In Chapter 5, we develop models on an individual basis utilising the above format.

3.5 Conclusion

In this chapter we have attempted to start to put together some of the strands of analysis developed in the previous two chapters. In doing so we have analysed the constraints and conditioning forces which shape and limit the investment decision of life offices and have examined their objective(s). We have argued that the maximisation of expected yields, subject to the life office being in a position to meet its contractual obligations, is perhaps a realistic unitary objective, particularly as life offices have in the present investment climate been forced to pay particular attention to their portfolio performance. We have argued that the investment decision is hierarchical in that the strategic or higher level decisions decide the portfolio mix and therefore the allocation of funds to the chosen classes of assets and the switching between these. The operational decisions (or tactical decisions) are the lower order choices of assets and switching within asset classes.

Although life offices, in common with other financial intermediaries, have to pay considerable attention to their liability structure, because they offer a long-term guarantee, they cannot change the terms on business already accepted and in consequence this has led life office managers to pay particular attention to capital security and later (in the face of low interest rates) income security. Bailey's canons for instance (as originally specified) concentrated attention on capital security and later the matching and immunisation approaches stressed the importance of being insulated against interest rate movements. Both approaches offered rather different solutions to the problem but both stressed the importance of liability structure in determining investment decisions. The Bailey concern for capital security could, if followed to its logical conclusions, lead to insolvency and the matching/immunisation approach, whilst a broad strategy to follow, cannot be applied universally by virtue of the growth of new business *and* pressure to increase yield. With the considerable movements in yields, particularly in marketable securities, profits are to be made from successful forecasting and trading and as we have seen from Chapter 2, this involves not just the allocation of new funds.

We focused attention on the strategic choice and allocation decisions among competing assets rather than the operational choice within asset classes which mean variance analysis can handle. We illustrated how we can utilise standard demand theory to derive asset demand functions which contain many of the sort of points that we have made in this and earlier chapters. Yields, constraints (such as income and market) can be incorporated and the models can be set within 'stock and flow' formulations. It is this set of demand equations that have been used by other researchers and in the next chapter we will see their practical value.

Notes

1. Some life offices did face extreme difficulties following the collapse of the property and stock market prices. These offices were particularly concerned with guaranteed income bonds. Liquidations have revealed apparent unsatisfactory situations in relation to the law on insurance companies. With offices becoming insolvent the long-term policy-holders become merely unsecured creditors entitled to prove for a capital sum which is equal to that of the value of their policies at the date of liquidation. There has been resistance from the 'stronger' life offices to the establishing of a fund to protect policy-holders who take the risk of insuring with weak offices. Nor will the government even give complete

protection against default at present. It was this divergence of views between government and the industry which led to the rather inadequate Policy-holders' Protection Act, 1975.

2. This has been more formally developed by A.D. Roy (142) where a portfolio return, R_i, would be set in terms of a disaster level which had to be avoided. In terms of the discussion in the previous chapter, this would be c^p.

3. Some qualitative evidence is available for the way life offices compete in the disclosure of new business data.

4. We are ignoring the issue of growth through merger. Concentration in the industry is covered in G. Clayton (30), R.L. Carter (25), P.J. Franklin and C. Woodhead (61).

5. For example achieved compound interest rates on endowment assurances maturing after a term of years. For a recent illustration of this see *The Economist* (54). These rates reflect managerial decisions taken over many years and perhaps are of little use for 'present-day' comparisons. However, J.R. Hemsted (78) did attempt to produce a year-by-year measure of overall performance and clearly this is possible for offices disclosing market value of assets in their reports and accounts.

6. For example, utilising other indices as proxies for investors' expectations. This is a perfectly legitimate exercise as they may be important indicators in their own right on which investment decisions are made.

7. For an analysis of expectations responses from interviews and questionnaires see B.G. Malkiel (100) and E.J. Kane and B.G. Malkiel (89).

8. The Bank of England (6) have argued that the expectations of investors in the gilt-edged market are extrapolative. See also C.A.E. Goodhart (69).

9. One approach has been to use random portfolios to provide a standard of comparison for measuring portfolio performance (see for example I. Friend *et al.* (64). The managed fund is compared with the random one and the difference in performance should reflect the efficiency of the investment decisions that have been made by the managed office fund. Another method has been suggested by E.A. Fox (60), J.A. Sieff (150) and the Society of Investment Analysts (155), in the form of establishing a 'control' fund. The control fund is invested in a fixed choice of securities and performance is compared with the actual fund. The final method used to develop an overall performance measurement which is an amalgam of the various investment decisions discussed earlier. Indices of these factors are compiled so as to identify the contribution made by the various types of investment decisions to the measured rate of return. This sort of procedure is still in its early stage of development, but it is more oriented to the practical side of investment policy and is not amenable to empirical testing. For further discussion of performance appraisal see G. Cocks (34) (35) and in pension funds, G.M. Lindley (97).

10. This finds support in A. Munro (110) which we discuss in Chapter 4. However, L.D. Jones' (88) study for the USA is based on the premise 'that it's flows alone which count' (p. 524).

11. However, in Chapter 2 we did illustrate the turnover within quarters. But there is a large degree of variation in the preferences over following an active or passive investment policy.

12. If we make the assumption (following F. de Leeuw (42) and subsequently A. Munro (110)) that the demand functions are homogeneous of degree one in money values then we would have $NA_i/\Sigma NA_i$ where ΣNA_i is total net acquisitions. The justification for this is that it is difficult to isolate any wealth effect from the influence of a variety of other trend factors.

13. Whilst in the main the relationships may be assumed to be linear and therefore readily estimatable, this need not be the case. The model of A.D. Roy (142) is an illustration of this.

14. The demand equations in the model are subject to restrictions namely that if the life office increases the proportion of its funds in one asset, it must be at the expense of proportions in the others. The other restriction is that the total net acquisitions (ΣNA_i), are equal to the total inflow of funds – that life offices do remain fully invested – if only in some short-term assets. It is by virtue of the balance sheet constraint that any one of the assets (or liabilities if they are to be estimated), becomes a residual asset.

4 THE EMPIRICAL EVIDENCE ON INVESTMENT BEHAVIOUR

4.1 Introduction

Although we may have cleared away some of the undergrowth surrounding the investment process of life offices, we are still left with the task of attempting to capture as much of this as we can in an empirical analysis. In this chapter we review the available work for the UK, though as we have already mentioned, there is little published work available. This contrasts very much with that published in the USA.[1] That is not to say that there has been no concern in the UK[2] for the way that life offices invest their funds, but that outside the actuarial journals, little academic interest has been generated since the important synthesis of investment principles given in the G. Clayton and W.T. Osborn (33) book published in 1965.

4.2 The UK Empirical Evidence

We can divide this evidence into two groupings. The first group contains studies which do not carry out full econometric specification and testing of life offices behaviour, but do some statistical analysis and here we refer to G. Clayton and W.T. Osborn (33) and R.L. Carter and J.E.V. Johnson (27). The second group of studies are those which do attempt complete models, and here again there are only two published studies, namely those of T.M. Ryan (144) and A. Munro (110), and an unpublished micro study by M.H.H. El-Habishi (55). We shall commence by analysing the first group of studies and because of the divergence in coverage we cannot offer any unifying approach.

4.2.1 General Studies

The Clayton and Osborn study had the objective of identifying, formulating and discussing the principles that underlie life office investment behaviour. We have already referred to this aspect of their study in Chapter 3 but in this present chapter we wish to focus attention on the statistical analysis they undertook. They did not, however (and neither was it their objective to), carry out an econometric specification and testing. Their statistical work was carried out on a cross-section basis for 1955 on the relationship between the size of insurance company (as indicated by total assets) and the percentage of assets held in seven asset types — mortgages, loans, British government securities, debentures, preference shares, ordinary shares and property. The study used data on industrial, proprietary life (predominantly small companies) mutual, composite offices and all of the sample of 86 life offices together. Whilst this study is both a disaggregated one and for a time period outside our own data period, we do feel that it is instructive to quote some of the Clayton and Osborn results (see Table 4.1), because they might give us some insight into the relationships between different assets in life office portfolios.

Table 4.1: Clayton and Osborn Results (Total Sample)

			Correlation coefficients 1955				
1	2	3	4	5	6	7	8
Total 86 life companies							
1	−.10	−.40*	−.44*	−.40*	−.35*	+.05	−.10
2		+.08	+.16	−.11	−.04	−.11	−.11
3			−.06	+.04	−.12	−.29*	+.06
4				+.24*	+.20	−.24*	+.13
5					+.46*	−.07	−.01
6						+.06	+.06
7							+.11
8							

Variables used

1. Mortgages as % of assets
2. Loans %
3. British government and guaranteed securities
4. Debentures %
5. Preference %
6. Ordinary %
7. Property %
8. Total assets in £ m
* Denotes statistical significance

Source: G. Clayton and W.T. Osborn (33) p. 264.

The highest correlation between size (given by total assets) and any of the asset classes was only 0.13. The most consistent results were negative correlations between mortgages and British government securities (−0.40), debentures (−0.44), preference shares (−0.40) and ordinary shares (−0.35). British government securities and debentures were also both negatively related to property −0.29 and −0.24 respectively. In addition there were consistent positive correlations between debentures and preference shares (0.24) and preference-equity (0.46). The authors did not place very much emphasis on these results and in fact, they are found in an Appendix to their book. Apart from the obvious criticism of the limitations of the particular statistical analysis used, it is not surprising that the results show little relationship. They were for a period when the portfolios of life offices were in a state of flux, not having fully recovered from the portfolio imbalance of the Second World War, nor had all companies adjusted to the changed investment environment which included investment in equity, property and other assets which previously were regarded with some displeasure.

The second study in this group is the quite recent work of R.L. Carter and J.E.V. Johnson (27). Their unpublished paper, apart from illustrating the relevant stock and flow magnitudes of life offices portfolios (including a brief examination of the range of different portfolio proportions that some life offices maintain), that we have ourselves dealt with on an aggregate basis in Chapter 2, focused on the activity or trading of life offices. They go on to suggest that life offices are concerned with a more active investment policy and therefore *not* with a policy to hold. The other main conclusion of the study is the importance that life offices play in the new issue market for company securities. This point has been made and tested by J.C. Dodds (49) (50) and others. They estimated for 1962-75 a linear and a log linear relationship for the net acquisitions of ordinary shares and the new issues and net acquisitions of debentures and issues, respectively, and what emerges is that there is a strong causal statistical relationship between net acquisitions and new issues of securities. What Carter and Johnson identified, however, was that in the case of debentures, '. . . when issues of debentures [X] are relatively small life offices will tend to purchase a large share of these (76% when X = £1m) but as the amount issued in any one year increases their share will decrease (38% when X = £100m)' (p. 10). Of course a major limitation (which they recognise) with this sort of work is that there are no means of identifying how much of the net acquisitions are actually new issues, because of course the net acquisitions data cover both the purchase of new and existing securities.

4.2.2 Econometric Studies

In this subsection we wish to discuss the published study of T.M. Ryan (144) and the unpublished study of A. Munro (110). They both attempt to model investment behaviour over fairly similar time periods, and given that they represent the only econometric studies available at this moment, we need to appraise them from the standpoint of our various discussions in earlier chapters which have laid the foundations for an understanding of the behavioural underpinnings of investment policy. We will deal with the two models in turn for ease of exposition and then offer an overall appraisal.

The T.M. Ryan (144) (145) study represents the only published econometric study of UK life offices behaviour. The purpose of the study was to attempt to develop a general model of portfolio review, as well as to offer background evidence on life company portfolio behaviour. In essence this might be seen as its strength in that an existing and established corpus of theory was being applied to an investing group which could be conceived as behaving in the necessary assumed fashion. Equally so, the model could, with minor alterations, be utilised, one presumes, to test the investment behaviour of other groups such as pension funds and the like. We would argue on the basis of our discussions in previous chapters that this generalist approach in fact is a crucial weakness of the Ryan model. In effect we argued in Chapter 3 that there would appear to be a number of factors which condition (and even constrain) investment behaviour and we discussed the objective(s) likely to motivate the offices. We can now proceed therefore to examine the Ryan approach against the backcloth of these internal and external constraints and the operative objective. We make use of Table 4.2 which details these for the two models in this sub-section.

The objective underlying the Ryan approach is that of expected yield maximisation. The life office is assumed to have a desired portfolio[3] of the form discussed earlier in Chapter 3 where the assets in question in the desired portfolio and the corresponding yields are for seven asset classes: (1) British government securities; (2) local authority loans; (3) debentures; (4) preference shares; (5) ordinary shares; (6) loans and mortgages; (7) land, property and ground rent. The data period runs from 1963 (1) to 1971 (4). The model underlying the study is a speculative one, and in consequence, he is adopting a more extreme position by having a model which allows for substitutability across the whole portfolio, although he has the necessary income (or wealth) constraint with the inflow of funds. Adjustment to the desired portfolio is not within a single period and the sole cause[4] for this he argues is the imperfectly competitive financial markets. In this Ryan is therefore taking account of one of our external constraints as specified in Table 4.3, namely that of market constraints, though he assigns the imperfection to the 'dominance' of life offices. As we indicated in Chapter

Table 4.2: Empirical Studies in the UK

	T.M. Ryan	A. Munro
Data period	1963 (1) — 1974 (4)	1963 (1) — 1972 (4)
Objective	yield maximisation	yield maximisation
Stock-flow framework	partial stock adjustment	flow of funds
Asset groupings	7 (BGs LA D Ps Os LM LPGR)	5 (PdSD PsSD OS LqA)
Expected yield formulation	1. distributed lag 2. 3 qkt moving average 3. perfect foresight	1. proxies 2. de Leeuw lag
Estimator used	OLS	OLS
Normalised	No	Yes
INTERNAL CONSTRAINTS		
Link with liability structure	No	Yes
Capital and income risk taken account of	No	Yes — via segmentation of portfolio
Liquidity consideration	No	Yes
Admin. and org. limits	No	No
EXTERNAL CONSTRAINTS		
Government regulation	No	No
Taxation	No	No
Exchange rate	No	No
Supply and market constraints	Yes	Yes
Inflation	No	No

Notes

BGs = British government securities; LA = Local authority securities; D = Debentures; Ps = Preference shares; OS = Ordinary shares; LM = Loans and mortgages; LPGR = Land property and ground rents; PdSD = Private sector debt; PsSD = Public sector debt; LqA = Liquid assets.

2, it is difficult to be assertive about the various facets that there are to dominance; holdings, trading and net acquisitions. This is particularly so given the importance of new issues to life offices, and the fact that the turnover data provided in Chapter 2 did indicate an ability to make quite significant adjustments in gilt-edged holdings and to a lesser extent in other securities. (See R.L. Carter and J.E.V. Johnson (27) and J.C. Dodds (49) for further coverage of this.) In consequence then the emphasis placed by Ryan is in our view misplaced, though we would agree that the sheer volume of holdings would militate against *wholesale* switching period by period.

On the internal constraints which we discussed in Chapter 3, and we detail in Table 4.2, the Ryan model takes little, if any, account of these factors. Whilst this omission could be perhaps accepted in the case of the majority of the external considerations, this is less defensible for the internal influences. There is no link with the liability structure, no discussion of the capital and income risk as they affect securities. Implicitly he is assuming that either securities are alike in the models that he presents, or that they can be treated as broad substitutes. Liquidity considerations are ignored and there is no equation to estimate liquid assets. Finally administration and organisation limits are only discussed implicitly in terms of the use of expected yields (which we will refer to later).

Whilst Ryan specifies a speculative model, he did not follow this through to allow for cross-substitution and to test for the substitute-complement pattern as only the own yield was included. The reasoning for this was to remove multi-collinearity. However, this omission of the vector of $\bar{y}_t$ asset yields is a serious weakness of the model. The three models presented by Ryan differ in the specification of the own yield term. In model one he uses a distributed lag formulation as a proxy of expected yield. In model two a three-quarter moving average of past yields and in model three a 'perfect foresight' variant is used. If we take these three models *seriatim* then the mechanism used to generate the $\bar{y}_t$ was of the form

$$\bar{y}_{it} = \sum_{j=1}^{\infty} \lambda_i^j y_{i,t-j} \quad \text{where } 0 < \lambda_i < 1 \tag{4.1}$$

Table 4.3 (a) gives the results for this particular model. Although the coefficients would appear to have the correct signs, little credence can be given to these results in that few of the coefficients are statistically significant. The speed of adjustment contained in the $x_{i,t-1}$ coefficients appeared broadly to confirm Ryan's *a priori* reasoning that the degree

Table 4.3: Asset Demand Functions: T.M. Ryan's Models

(a) Quarterly 1963-1971, Model One

	Constant	$\Delta \bar{y}_{it}$	w_t	$x_{i,t-1}$	$\bar{R}^2$
British government securities	−71.68* (30.33)	0.03 (4.17)	0.57* (0.14)	0.20 (0.15)	0.51
Local authority loans	−7.96 (4.95)	1.76* (0.67)	0.03 (0.02)	0.16 (0.18)	0.28
Debentures	−18.15 (17.65)	4.16 (2.17)	0.14* (0.07)	0.57* (0.14)	0.44
Preference shares	−15.72* (4.23)	1.59* (0.55)	0.05* (0.02)	0.57* (0.13)	0.70
Ordinary shares	−13.94 (14.34)	0.26 (1.37)	0.19* (0.08)	0.49* (0.16)	0.46
Loans and mortgages	−2.44 (14.72)	1.84 (1.42)	0.02 (0.05)	0.77* (0.14)	0.51
Land, property, ground rents	1.46 (5.42)	0.60 (1.01)	0.03 (0.03)	0.81* (0.10)	0.76

Figures in brackets are standard errors.
* Denotes significance at the 5% level.

of imperfection would be highest in markets where secondary markets were thin or virtually non-existent. On this basis he felt it would be low for British government securities (in this case 0.20) and higher for loans and mortgages (0.77) and land, property and ground rents (0.81). But whilst this may be the case, will the imperfection in markets which is determined by the dominance of life funds necessarily follow this pattern? Without an analysis of the adjustment link between dominance in markets and speed of adjustment, it is not possible to be specific because the coefficient will include some of the effects of dominance. From our previous analysis, it is more significant in the market for debentures, as well as internal adjustment costs attributable to the search for, and evaluation of, investment opportunities. Additionally, there may be constraints on the supply side of markets.

In this model the sum of the bs on the w_t term sums to 1.03 and this would appear to justify, more or less, the balance sheet constraint

Table 4.3 (cont.)

(b) Comparison of Expected-yield Coefficients in Model One and Model Two

	$\Delta \hat{y}_1$	$\Delta \hat{y}_2$	$\Delta \hat{y}_3$	$\Delta \hat{y}_4$	$\Delta \hat{y}_5$	$\Delta \hat{y}_6$	$\Delta \hat{y}_7$
Model One	0.03 (4.17)	1.76* (0.67)	4.16 (2.17)	1.59* (0.55)	0.26 (1.37)	1.84 (1.42)	0.60 (1.01)
Model Two	−0.80 (23.66)	−2.35 (3.33)	−11.86 (10.50)	1.53 (2.55)	−2.41 (5.53)	14.81 (12.12)	0.09 (0.12)

Figures in brackets are standard errors.
* Denotes signifiance at the 5% level.

(c) Model Three — Perfect Foresight

	Constant	$\Delta \hat{y}_{it}$	w_t	$x_{i,t-1}$	$\bar{R}^2$
British government securities	−71.63* (20.87)	0.84 (16.34)	0.57* (0.12)	0.20 (0.17)	0.51
Local authority loans	−0.31 (4.49)	−1.14 (2.49)	0.005 (0.025)	0.35 (0.18)	0.11
Debentures	2.34 (14.58)	−4.18 (7.63)	0.079 (0.067)	0.64* (0.15)	0.37
Preference shares	−6.34 (2.86)	2.02 (1.78)	0.032* (0.016)	0.82* (0.12)	0.63
Ordinary shares	−11.81 (12.86)	−0.79 (4.06)	0.177* (0.079)	0.49* (0.18)	0.46
Loans and mortgages	15.56 (9.85)	0.99 (7.49)	−0.027 (0.041)	0.65* (0.15)	0.52
Land, property, ground rents	0.46 (5.33)	0.04 (0.07)	0.033 (0.033)	0.82* (0.10)	0.76

Figures in brackets are standard errors.
* Denotes significance at the 5% level.

Source: T.M. Ryan (144).

that the available cash inflow is allocated to the asset set. Two points can be made here. In the first place if he has used net inflow of new funds as his proxy for Δw_t, then summing the coefficients on w_t over all equations would *not* produce an answer of unity because the net acquisitions of any security is affected not just by net new funds, but by the availability of funds from the sale of other assets. As over this period, life funds were at times net sellers of some securities, particularly local authority securities and preference shares (see Table A.2 (a)), then these additional funds could be and were used for investment in alternative assets. It is, therefore, surprising that given the net sales of these two assets over a large part of this period, the positive signs were noted on the coefficients of the Δw_t variable. The second reason we can advance is that short-term assets have been excluded as an asset class, presumably on the basis they are held for transactions purposes. But unless Ryan adjusted the accruing funds to take account of short-term assets, again the coefficients on Δw_t in the system of asset-demand equations would not sum to unity.

In model two the expected yield variable was respecified as we have seen by using a three-quarter moving average of past yields. The justification for this was that Ryan felt that a quarter by quarter planning horizon was too short for life companies. In fact this respecification appeared to make little difference apart from the coefficients on the $\Delta \bar{y}_t$ and there were sign changes and the standard errors deteriorated. Table 4.3 (b) gives the comparison for $\bar{y}_t$ between model 1 and model 2.

For model 3 Ryan abandoned auto-regressive methods for generating forecasts of yields on the basis that they could not take account of the welter of information (some qualitative) which would go into a forecast. He proposed a perfect foresight model where anticipated yields were proxied by actual yields, so that the yield achieved in $t + 1$ is the rate in t expected to hold in $t = 1$. In other words the investment managers in the industry as a whole can make perfect forecasts. The rationale for this approach, as Ryan points out in his 'Rejoinder' (145) is that the skills that investment managers have may lead them to make better forecasts than those generated by an auto-regressive scheme. If we were also to consider the dominance that Ryan argues is present in financial markets then the actions of life investment managers may well bring about the course of events which they had expected. In fact, as the results show (in Table 4.3 (c)), this formulation does not produce any meaningful results and we can observe that this formulation of the expected yield is the worst of the three models.

Ryan recognised the limitations and deficiencies of his results and argued that this may be attributable to two possible factors. The first referred to the use of the 'own yield' as the only yield variable in the equations and the second to his choice of the planning horizon over which investment managers review their portfolio in the light of their expectations or views as to the future trends of yields. We shall return to discussing the Ryan model after we have surveyed the A. Munro (110) model. At which time we can then appraise, overall, how the two approaches answer the questions we feel are important from our previous discussions in evaluating and explaining the portfolio behaviour of life offices.

The second econometric study we report on for the UK is an unpublished paper by A. Munro (110). Whereas the Ryan methodology was to use a general model of portfolio review, the Munro study was an attempt to estimate for the life insurance industry its investment behaviour with a view to incorporating this into a 'flow of funds' model of the whole financial sector. Flows are thus given primacy of place. The purpose of specifying such large-scale financial models is both to understand more of the workings of the financial system *per se* and to assist in the respecification of the financial sector of more general macro-economic models. Munro in his model certainly attempted to include those factors which he felt conditioned investment behaviour.

If we refer to Table 4.2, then we see that with regard to the internal constraints he had a direct link to the liability structure. Additionally he took account of the differing nature of assets by suggesting a segmentation of the balance sheet. Liquidity he handled by attempting to measure those liquid funds necessary for the normal life office business and then he estimated the net acquisition of the adjusted liquid assets (what he referred to as excess liquid assets). In part, too, we can say that he attempted to recognise one of the external conditioning forces in the form of supply or market constraints. By entering new issues of corporate debt he is explicitly recognising a supply constraint. He also raised the question of the 'dominant' position life offices may have in particular markets. However, he did not utilise this formally in his model, though he did give an illustration of how the observed investment behaviour may have produced the movements in the actual investment rates.

There are marked differences in the model proposed by Munro compared to those we have seen that Ryan used. He faced the same problem though of specifying the relevant expected yield data and he used a mixture[5] of proxies and extrapolative mechanisms. One final problem in asset yields he does cover is their collinearity. Ryan we can recall simply used own-yield responses to remove this problem. Munro, following W.L. Silber (151), overcomes this multi-collinearity by using the interest rate differentials (in model 2) between the gilt and local authority rates.

Turning away from the yields to the assets themselves, five asset groupings were identified: public sector debt (which is an amalgam of government securities and local authority debt); private sector debt (debentures, preference shares and loans and mortgages); equity (ordinary shares and unit trust units); property and liquid assets. The criterion used by Munro for aggregation was for the assets to be subject to the same type of risk (and hence likely to experience high collinearity in return) to be grouped together. Whilst A. Leijonhufvud (95) gives a fuller discussion of aggregation criteria, the Munro classification is satisfactory. In essence what the five groupings produce are assets which provide liquidity, assets which may be expected to provide a hedge against inflation (equity and property) and assets whose return is fixed in nominal terms but which offer marketability and are default free (public sector securities). Some commentators would argue that local authority securities are technically not default free and would point to the historically higher interest rates on debt instruments of comparable type to those of the central government. M. Craig (38), however, argues that they should be regarded as equivalent and seeks other explanations of this yield gap.

The data period covered in this study (1963 (1) to 1972 (4)) is slightly longer than that of Ryan and the same estimator, OLS, is used. Three models are tested each referring to a different form of investment allocation. The first is that the investment process takes the form of a simultaneous allocation across the five asset groupings so that all five are potential substitutes for the net new funds available for investment. In this approach he is broadly following the Ryan methodology; though as we have argued already the explanatory variables in the equations presented differ markedly.

The other two hypotheses are that the investment process follows a sequential pattern whereby the investment manager follows a two-part process (in model 2) and a three-part process (in model 3). In the former, property investment in each period is assumed to be predetermined and the remaining funds are then allocated on a simultaneous basis. In the three-part process, property is again predetermined, then private sector debt takes a prior call and the remaining funds are then allocated to public sector debt, equity and liquid assets simultaneously. The results presented for the three models were the 'best' estimates of each hypothesis. Each equation was estimated on an individual basis and various variables discarded so that only when he was satisfied with equations for each investment group did he then estimate the equations using the same set of explanatory variables.

Taking the models *seriatim*, model 1 reveals a mixture of results (see Table 4.4 (a)). Overall, the fits are moderately good with the highest $\bar{R}^2$ of 0.78 for private sector debt and 0.63 for equity. It would appear that most of the variables do have the correct sign, though in some cases the coefficients are insignificant at the 5 per cent level and this is to be expected given the cross-effects of interest rate terms, a finding confirmed in the USA by B. Bosworth and J.S, Duesenberry (15). But in the equations where *a priori* one would expect the influence of particular variables to be strong, in general the coefficients have the correct sign and are statistically significant at the 5 per cent level.

If we focus attention on the four equations separately we find that for equity (equation 3), the coefficients on the expected level of GDP and the proportion of index-linked policies (to total inflow of funds) both have the correct sign and are significant. The rationale here is that the prospects for shares will be linked with movements of the income which GDP measures. The linked policies are, in the main, policies (as we saw in Chapters 1 and 2) linked to the purchase of equities (or property) and therefore we would expect this variable to assume some importance in the equations (although such policies were only recorded in the data series after 1970). The sign on the net issues of long-term corporate bonds is also to be expected in that issues of debentures are only contemplated when business conditions (and share prices) are booming. But the coefficient is not significant.

In the case of the public sector debt equation (number 1), it would appear that the extrapolative mechanism for interest rates has performed quite well with the correct sign and is significant; confirming perhaps that as long-term yields rise (with consequent falls in prices and capital market loss on the existing portfolio) a smaller proportion is invested. The excess liquid asset variable is significant and its sign is suggestive that excess liquid assets of a previous period are utilised to invest in public sector securities (the sign is also suggestive of this for private sector debt, but the coefficient is not statistically significant). This would suggest that perhaps public sector debt is a residual asset or a depository for unallocated funds and this, in part, supports a view expressed earlier in Chapter 2 of this study. If we also look at the liquid asset equation, we see that when liquid assets are high in relation to total inflow in one period, the next period sees a lower proportion

Table 4.4: Life Insurance Investment Behaviour — 1963 (1) to 1972 (4) — A. Munro's Study

(a) Model 1

	Constant	Ex GDP	$RGB^\theta(K_2)$	$(RLA-RGB)_{-1}$	BS LIQ%	$XL_{t-1}/TNIP$	ILLF/TNIP	ΔLLTIC/TNIP	$\bar{R}^2$	D.W.
1. ΔLLTGLP/TNIP	-0.177	0.018	-0.168		0.020	0.557	-0.100	0.137	0.34	1.6
	(0.56)	(0.91)	(2.49)		(1.06)	(3.08)	(0.36)	(1.17)		
2. ΔLLTPLP/TNIP	1.09	0.019	-0.020		-0.058	0.060	-0.413	-0.437	0.78	1.54
	(5.07)	(1.47)	(0.43)		(4.46)	(0.48)	(2.18)	(5.44)		
3. ΔEQLP/TNIP	-0.139	0.030	0.059		0.016	-0.022	0.561	0.092	0.63	1.60
	(0.75)	(2.67)	(1.49)		(1.46)	(0.20)	(3.46)	(1.34)		
4. ΔLIQ/TNIP	-0.175	-0.035	0.161		0.031	-0.64	-0.269	0.23	0.39	2.0
	(0.69)	(2.26)	(2.97)		(2.09)	(4.42)	(1.22)	(2.45)		

(b) Model 2

	Constant	Ex GDP	$RGB^\theta(K_2)$	$(RLA-RGB)_{-1}$	BS LIQ%	XL_{t-1}/TNI	ILLF/TNI	ΔLLTIC/TNI	$\bar{R}^2$	D.W.
1.	0.133	0.009	-0.228	-0.25	0.003	0.567	-0.081	0.117	0.36	1.51
	(0.25)	(0.34)	(2.75)	(0.62)	(0.09)	(3.11)	(0.27)	(1.01)		
2.	1.39	0.015	-0.025	-0.005	-0.073	0.063	-0.381	-0.447	0.78	1.55
	(3.73)	(0.78)	(0.44)	(0.19)	(3.3)	(0.5)	(1.87)	(5.55)		
3.	0.083	0.02	0.055	-0.021	0.006	-0.037	0.563	0.078	0.58	1.72
	(0.26)	(1.28)	(1.12)	(0.88)	(0.32)	(0.34)	(3.29)	(1.15)		
4.	-0.611	-0.044	0.199	0.051	0.064	-0.594	-0.102	0.25	0.42	2.01
	(1.43)	(2.05)	(3.02)	(1.60)	(2.54)	(4.1)	(0.44)	(2.75)		

Table 4.4 (cont.)

(c) Model 3

					XL_{t-1}/TAF	ILLF/TAF		
1.	0.594 (3.94)	−0.018 (0.4)	−0.382 (2.61)		−0.02 (0.284)	−0.298 (2.49)	0.37	1.83
2.	1.38 (5.53)			−0.074 (5.12)		−0.507 (8.81)	0.77	1.32
3.	−0.173 (1.67)	0.099 (3.3)	0.072 (0.71)		0.586 (12.18)	0.886 (10.75)	0.95	1.24
4.	0.579 (5.12)	−0.082 (2.49)	0.31 (2.82)		−0.566 (10.81)	−0.588 (6.55)	0.91	1.89

t values are in the brackets below the coefficients they refer to.

Key to variables

1. ΔLLTGLP: net investment in public sector debt; 2. ΔLLTPLP: net investment in private sector debt; 3. ΔEQLP: net investment in equity; 4. ΔLIQ: net investment in liquid assets; TNIP: total investment (items 1-4 + property); TNI: the total of items 1, 2, 3 and 4; TAF: the total of items 1, 3 and 4; Ex GDP: expected rate of growth of GDP (NIER forecasts); RGB^e(K$_2$): extrapolative expectation of gilt rate.

Sources: A. Munro (110) Tables A, B and C.

invested in this category of assets. This result would not be confirmed, however, for the period 1974/5 when extreme uncertainty about many securities markets led to an abnormal build-up of liquid assets.

Turning to the private sector debt equation (number 2), overall it appears quite well specified and it is interesting to note that the coefficient on the new issue of corporate bonds is correctly signed (it is negative as the variable is entered with a negative sign) and statistically significant. The building society liquidity ratio (in $t - 1$) coefficient is also statistically significant and it would appear also to have the correct sign (i.e. negative) in that when liquidity is low in building societies, any excess demand in the mortgage market may force borrowers into other avenues for housing funds including life companies. This may be the case if an expectation of a further rise in house prices is a motivator. The hypothesis is appealing in that those persons who are contemplating house purchase via a life office are not likely to be the marginal house buyers that building societies would refuse in a mortgage famine.

We illustrate the results for model 2 in Table 4.4 (b). This model differs from model 1 in two main respects. The available funds for investment are reduced by the amount of predetermined property investment in the period. The second difference is that the differential between the local authority 3-month rate and the 20-year gilt rate (both levels) lagged one period is used in all four equations. There is little difference between the two models in either explanatory power or of the statistical significance of the coefficients, though in the equity equation, EXGDP is no longer significant. The inclusion of the interest differential term did little to improve the equations, though it has the correct sign for public sector debt and for liquid assets, though neither coefficient was statistically significant. It is of course understandable that this second model is so little different from model 1 because the property equation was never estimated in model 1.

In model 3 (portrayed in Table 4.4 (c)), the three-part sequential process of investment is tested. The overall fit of two equations improves for equity (0.95) and liquid assets (0.91), though the Durbin-Watson (DW) statistic which tests for auto-correlation worsens in both cases. The fit on the other two equations differs only marginally, but there is some evidence of sign changing between the three formulations. For instance in the case of public sector debt, the sign on the excess liquid asset variable is now negative and the coefficient is no longer statistically significant. In the case of the demand for equity, the expected growth of GDP becomes significant (as in model 1) and for the excess liquid assets the sign is now positive and the coefficient statistically significant, suggesting that prior to an increase in the demand for equity, there is a build up of liquid assets to finance the acquisitions.

The model, by prescribing this three-part allocation process, denies the substitutability between private and public sector assets and similarly in the case of property, as it is predetermined before any other asset. The burden of cross influence would appear to rest with public sector debt and equity, both of which have well-developed secondary markets. But the assets differ markedly in the attributes they offer to investors. The inclusion of short-term assets in $t - 1$ is suggestive of liquid assets being a buffer which are built up for eventual investment in longer-term financial assets. In terms of model 3 these can only be equity as the public sector debt coefficient has a negative sign (though it is not significant) in model 3 and a positive sign (and is significant) in the other two models. Munro recognises the deficiencies of his approach in model 3 because cross influences are excluded and he suggests that the proportions of private sector debt could be entered in equations 2-4 as an independent variable and likewise the proportion of investment in property.

Throughout all the three models the fit and the significance of the coefficients in the public sector debt equation do not improve. This is a disappointing feature, particularly given the significance that government securities have in the portfolios of life offices. What is perhaps important, however, is that the extrapolative expectations variable for long-term gilts $RGB^e(K_2)$ performs quite well in the public sector demand equations. In all three models it appears correctly signed and significant and this is in line with a finding by W.E. Norton (113) for the public's demand for government securities over the period 1955 (2) to 1966 (2). Yet the interpretation of what this extrapolative mechanism actually means is open to question as Munro rightly argues. If we can presume over the data period that the rate is exogenous to the life offices and determined by the monetary authorities, then the presumption is that as the rate increases (and prices fall) life offices reduce their demand. The Ryan approach presumed, however, that the rate was materially affected by activities of life offices themselves. Munro recognised that this may be the case particularly after 1972 when the official policy in the gilt market changed. However, even for the period of this model, when official policy was one of 'leaning into the wind', the market rate was inevitably a combination of official policy and reactions of investors.

4.3 Conclusion

These two studies represent the only econometric work on life office investment behaviour *per se* in the UK. We now ask ourselves how they answer the questions we posed in Chapters 2 and 3. The Munro and Ryan approaches differ materially yet their data periods overlap all but for one year (Ryan's is 1963-71 and Munro's 1963-72). Each approach presents a different set of asset demand equations so that only in the case of equity can any direct comparison be made of them on an equation by equation basis. Ryan, we recall, specified seven asset demand equations neglecting liquid assets, whilst Munro has grouped some of the assets together into broader categories.

The Ryan model was intended to be a general one applicable to other financial institutions and in this sense it abstracts somewhat from the behavioural underpinnings of life offices. Munro, on the other hand, devotes more consideration to these, but even here, the ultimate purpose was to place the model within a wider framework of a multi-asset/liability model and in this respect the choice of asset demand groupings was probably conditioned by the specification of this larger model. One of the obvious problems of pulling out individual sectors from a large integrated model for more detailed consideration with a view to placing them back into the model is that sacrifices have to be made in, for example, the level of aggregation used for financial claims.

The Munro approach allowed for shuffling (in model 1) across the whole portfolio (including liquid assets) and the allocation of funds is done simultaneously. So this speculative stance is similar in overall approach to Ryan, and this finds further support from D.G. Simonson (152) for mutual funds in the USA. Munro enters assets variables in ratio form and he explicitly attempts to take account of the yields on the assets in the eligible set either directly by the expected yield (as in the case of public sector securities), or by using a proxy for the yield. Having said that, the Munro model attempts to forge a link with the balance sheet by recognising that liquid assets may be built up in some periods and run down in others and therefore he does use an 'excess liquidity' variable to give that link. In addition he attempts to integrate the liability structure into the model, something we have argued for in Chapter 3. In his formulation he achieves this by using the growth in index-linked assurance as an independent variable. So we have in the Munro model an attempt at bringing together some element of hedging with speculative behaviour, though again we must stress he was emphasising the 'flows' nature of the process.

Ryan, as we have seen, presents three models, the difference being in the specification of the expected yields, whereas the Munro models differ in the actual modelling of the life office investment process. In doing so Munro tries to take account of the commitments of the previous periods which have to be met in another, later period. Hence we have the sequential process of fund allocation. This would appear to accord with some commentators' views, notably those of J.R.S. Revell (135) and it does improve the statistical fit of the equity and liquid asset equations. However, Munro would be the first to argue that these equations need further refinements to improve their specification. Yet he would appear to have captured some of the important influences on life offices' investment decisions.

So our judgement of the two approaches is that both leave a lot of questions unanswered, although they do take us some of the way in formulating a model of life offices behaviour. They both reveal the difficulties of formulating expected yields; they both illustrate the econometric difficulties of modelling such a varied portfolio. One which has such a large volume of funds to dispose of period by period and one from which it would appear active trading takes place. Perhaps the worrying feature of both models is the poor fit of the government securities equation, given the significance the market plays in life offices investment and the part life offices themselves play in this market. This is a particular issue we shall take up in Chapter 5.

Notes

1. See J.D. Cummins (39), L.D. Jones (88), J.E. Pesando (121) for overall models of behaviour and F.H. Shott (149), G.A. Bishop (13), D.B. Houston and R.M. Simon (85) for models of one or more aspects of their behaviour. For a descriptive account see A.F. Brimmer (19), D. McCahan (99), J.E. Walker (165) and Commission for Money and Credit Monograph (36).

2. See T.M. Titmuss (162), D.H. Robertson and S.R. Dennison (139), J. Johnston and G.W. Murphy (87) for early examples of this and the evidence to the Wilson Committee (168) for a modern viewpoint.

3. The Ryan notation was

$$x_t^* = a\mathcal{Y}_t + b w_t$$

where x_t is the desired portfolio, $\mathcal{Y}_t$ the vector of asset yields and w_t the wealth variable. It is not clear in the Ryan model whether the w_t refers to total net acquisitions or whether he adjusts the data for changes in the inherited portfolio to produce a series for net inflow of new funds, which is what he originally refers to as w_t. In addition he gives no indication as to where and what type of yield variables he uses. See J.C. Dodds (47).

4. He dismisses transactions costs and this is perhaps too sweeping given the fact that they are not uniform across assets in the portfolio.

5. The proxies used included the expected rate of growth of GDP for the

equity market and the building societies liquidity ratio for the mortgage market. For gilt-edged markets he used an extrapolative mechanism as portrayed in Equation 4.2 using a 20-year redemption yield (RGB) with weights used for the k of 0.25.

$$RGB^e(K_2) = RGB_t - \frac{1-k}{1-k''} \sum_{i=1}^{k} k^{i-1} RGB_{t-1} \tag{4.2}$$

A three-month local authority rate was also used for the liquid asset set.

5 MODELLING LIFE OFFICE INVESTMENT BEHAVIOUR: INDIVIDUAL DEMAND SPECIFICATIONS

5.1 Introduction

We have laid out the evidence in previous chapters on the portfolio composition of life companies and changes in this for the period 1963-76; the nature of their liabilities, the objectives which they are alleged to have and the various methods by which they may attempt to achieve these objectives. Additionally, we have summarised and criticised the evidence for the UK on the previous attempts to model their portfolio behaviour. In this chapter, we now wish to start the estimation of our own models, taking into account the various considerations already stressed elsewhere in this study. In this respect we wish to develop a framework which combines and synthesises the objectives of life companies with the environmental and institutional factors which condition their behaviour.

In attempting to model this investment behaviour we have essentially two choices (though not mutually exclusive) in the sample coverage. We can utilise an 'industry' level approach using aggregate time series data, with all the strictures that that may bring and/or we can adopt a 'micro' strategy of studying the investment behaviour of individual companies or group of companies (see for example L.S. Wehrle (167) for a study of life insurance in the USA and on a more general basis see D.D. Hester and J.L. Pierce (81) for a comparison of micro and macro approaches in US commercial and mutual banks). Ideally both approaches are to be preferred in that they are complementary. Micro studies permit a more in-depth analysis of investment intentions, particularly with regard to the sort of issues we discussed in Chapter 3 on objectives and constraints on these. However, these studies suffer from the difficulties of aggregation to obtain some general industry-wide conclusions. Macro studies do, however, offer this opportunity of explaining the activities of the whole sector within financial markets, but, unfortunately, aggregation brings sacrifices in terms of data sources, attitudes on investment policy and the like.

Our brief, as we have already stressed, is to follow an industry-wide approach. But given the limitations of the data, our ability to capture the full flavour of this investment process in models of behaviour will be constrained and indeed the results we do present in this chapter are not as good as we would like. They perhaps go some of the way in illustrating some of the key elements in the investment choice process. In Section 5.3 we offer individual demand specifications of six asset types. Whilst we appreciate that such a piecemeal approach can be criticised, as it can ignore the overall portfolio position, we do take account of this to some extent by positing a sequential investment allocation process. Additionally the advantages (as we see them) from these individual specifications outweigh the disadvantages; particularly as we are not constrained by strictures imposed by an aggregate model. In consequence we can attempt to explore more fully the possible effects on each demand. We recognise that in fitting the pieces of this jigsaw together (in Chapter 6) we will have to compromise and we accept that we may not be able to incorporate these specifications into a neat and comprehensive model, without some sacrifices.

5.2 Towards Individual Demand Specifications

Whilst the data period of our study is 1963 (1) to 1976 (4), in the estimation in this section we use data to 1974 (4) so that we can test (in Chapter 6) for the predictive power of the models outside of the data period used in the estimation. We need, however, at this stage to delineate the asset groupings which we attempt to explain for net acquisitions. We can recall that the Ryan and Munro treatments differed here and from our analysis of the data series in Chapter 2 we offer the following asset types:

1. Corporate bonds (debentures)
2. Ordinary shares (including unit trust units)
3. Government securities — overall and split by maturity range to focus on long bonds (of over fifteen years to maturity)
4. Loans and mortgages — overall and split to examine house purchase loans separately
5. Land, property and ground rents
6. Short-term assets.

Additionally a brief examination will be given to residual assets. These include overseas assets, local authority securities and preference shares.

Having listed these groupings we need to recall the various characteristics and attributes of these assets that we discussed in Chapter 2. In fact we can distinguish between (1) fixed interest (gilts and debentures) with variable capital values; (2) equity assets (ordinary shares and property) which have variable returns and capital values; (3) assets fixed in longer nominal money terms (loans and mortgages); and (4) short-term assets which will be fixed in nominal terms but by virtue of their maturity do not introduce questions of marketability.

If the portfolio strategy is to be framed in terms of deciding between these four asset groupings (with operational decisions to be taken within the groupings), then we need to appraise, on an overall basis, some of the factors which could influence these strategic decisions. We can now detail these factors to be four in number, namely:

1. changing liability structure and adjustment to the 'desired' portfolio
2. issues of stock
3. movements in yields and inflation trends
4. availability of funds — income constraint.

We will give an overview of these factors before we commence to include these in individual demand specifications.

We have already discussed the importance of liabilities in terms of the guarantees life offices give and importance that a broadly-based investment policy may have in relation to determining the portfolio strategy. We illustrated, for example, that fixed interest stocks can offer income security, whilst equity securities can give capital growth. One would presume, for instance, that a preponderance of annuities and single premium policies might lead to a greater interest in fixed interest and group pension business, greater interest in equities. In addition linked policies to ordinary shares or property give an immediate indication of portfolio needs. If the liability structure had not changed over our data period, then we could safely assume that whilst this structure would be a significant factor in moulding the strategic choices among the various asset classes, the allocation into these, period by period, would not change materially if the new business written was no different from that of previous periods. We have seen, however, that there has been some variability in new policies written and whilst these might not produce a significant change in the overall liability structure, we might expect them to have the sort of effect on the allocation basis mentioned above. It must be stressed, however, that to use these data in equations is to be questioned, as they are unsatisfactory measures of what might be actually available for investment, but they should offer some indication of trends. If life offices do have a target portfolio in mind, which can be reflected in terms of portfolio proportions, then the changes in the liability structures coupled with the other factors which go to make up this 'desired' portfolio can be handled from both the 'flow' and 'stock' aspects. The stock adjustment mechanism we specified in Chapter 3 and utilised in Chapter 4 by Ryan captures both influences and can be simplified to the use of a lagged dependent variable. We recognise, therefore, that the portfolio may thus be continuously in disequilibrium and not just for the market imperfections of 'dominance' ascribed by Ryan.

If the matching-immunisation viewpoints hold, then it is the liability structure which will dominate the choice of this desired portfolio and in the allocation of the new inflow of policy reserves, the main constraint will be from the supply side. Apart from the need to maintain a 'long' stance in markets in the face of the shortening which inevitably occurs with dated security through time, the trading which occurs will normally be within a given class of securities (e.g. within long bonds or with equities); what we referred to in Chapter 3 as operational switching. If the speculative viewpoint holds, then yields and other factors will assume greater importance, although emphasis might still be given to the allocation of the inflow of funds to achieve the necessary change, rather than attempting to make fundamental changes in the inherited stock position. Another factor that we would argue can be significant in portfolio strategic decision-making is the supply constraint, the availability of stock. This is to be recognised more where formal markets exist such as fixed interest and equity securities. Here 'issues' are made and the data are more or less readily available and we can test for the significance of these on the net acquisitions and we set out the results below in Table 5.1.

The results largely confirm the importance of new issues to life offices. This is also the case for pension funds in the equity market (see J.C. Dodds (49)). If we take the company securities first we can see that for corporate bonds and ordinary shares the results give a moderately good fit. The principal causal factor affecting the supply is the long-term economic progress of the nation, which will determine the needs of business firms for plant and machinery and for more permanent financing of working capital. The economy, of course, is subject to the short-term influences of the ups and downs in the business cycle which themselves reflect the ability of companies to make capital issues. An examination of the data on new issues of both debentures and ordinary shares would reveal this, with a bunching of issues in some periods and a dearth in others. Recall also that the work

Table 5.1: Net Acquisitions of Marketable Securities and Issues (1963-74)[d]

Variable	Dependent variable	Constant	I_t^C [a]	I_t^O [b]	I_t^G [c]	I_t^{GS}	I_t^{GM}	I_t^{GL}	$\bar{R}^2$	DW	Det. C
Equation number											
5.1 (1)	NA^C	13.6* (3.9)	0.23* (0.03)						0.5	1.3	1.0
5.1 (2)	NA^O	26.1* (6.3)		0.44* (0.08)					0.4	1.0	1.0
5.1 (3)	NA^G	31.4* (4.9)			0.07* (0.01)				0.4	1.6	1.0
5.1 (4)	NA^{GS}	-3.19 (2.5)				0.004 (0.01)			–	2.3	1.0
5.1 (5)	NA^{GM}	-2.14 (2.89)					0.05* (0.02)		0.1	1.4	1.0
5.1 (6)	NA^{GL}	15.2* (4.3)						0.2* (0.02)	0.7	1.9	1.0

Glossary:

NA^C net acquisitions of corporate bonds (debentures).[e]

NA^O, NA^G, NA^{GS} NA^{GM}, NA^{GL} net acquisitions of ordinary shares, total government securities, short dated (0-5) government, medium dated (5-15), long dated (15+ years) respectively.

I_t^C, I_t^O, I_t^G, I_t^{GS}, I_t^{GM}, I_t^{GL} issues of these assets respectively.

Notes:

a. For corporate bonds the data are loan capital net issues (excluding international issues) as published by the Bank of England.

b. For ordinary shares the data are also net issues and also from the Bank of England.

c. For government securities these data are not just new issues per se but include other stock provided by the government through the Bank of England.

d. We follow our standard practice of quoting the standard errors (in brackets under the coefficients). The asterisk denotes statistical significance at the 5 per cent level. $\bar{R}^2$ is the coefficient of determination adjusted for degrees of freedom. DW is the Durbin-Watson statistic used to test for serial correlation in the residuals but of course we recognise that the presence of a lagged dependent variable can bias the value towards 2.0. Det. C is the determinant of the zero order correlation matrix of the explanatory variables in each equation. It is a measure of multi-collinearity.

e. Data on gross purchases were also used, but the figures were disappointing. For example, for corporate bonds, a fit of only 23 per cent was achieved.

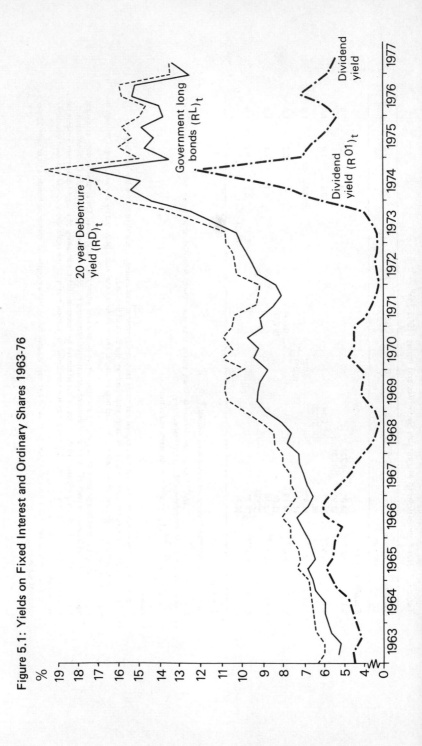

Figure 5.1: Yields on Fixed Interest and Ordinary Shares 1963-76

of R.L. Carter and J.E.V. Johnson (27) analyses this relationship arguing, for example, that in periods when issues of debentures were small
life offices would appear to purchase a relatively large share. It might be
thought that gross purchases of debentures would be determined by
new issues rather than net acquisition. This, however, was not the case
for whilst the coefficient on these issues was statistically significant, the
fit was only 23 per cent, as measured by $\bar{R}^2$, the coefficient of determination adjusted for degrees of freedom. For ordinary shares, on the
other hand, we might at first sight have expected a better fit, as some of
the new issues will be in the form of 'rights' issues and whilst shareholders can sell their rights, there is often the temptation to take these
up. On the other hand, as these issues data series include share exchanges
(to finance takeovers), then perhaps the fit we have achieved is about
what we might reasonably expect.

Turning to the gilt-edged market we can see that overall there is
a reasonably good fit in the 'all gilts' category and issues. On the
maturity split we can dismiss the shorts relationship as by and large
issues of so short securities are minimal. For the medium, the coefficient on issues is also statistically insignificant at the 5 per cent level
and the fit is virtually non-existent, probably for the same reason.
The longs equation has an excellent fit, though this is probably
not surprising given the revealed interest that life offices have in
the long market and the possibility of the tailoring of the debt by
the monetary authorities. (See for example W.T. Terrell and W.J. Fraser
(158).)

Whilst there are likely to be supply constraints on the other assets
(apart from possibly short-term assets), we cannot take account of this.
For loans and mortgages and property investment the availability will
depend on recommendations and localised search. Relationships with
agents and others can be important and this is often referred to as
'customer relations' (see D.R. Hodgman (84). Some of the property
investment will be the result of development programmes in which
life offices are participating, e.g. city centre developments, but certainly some of the other supply will come from auctions and introductions.

Turning to the question of movements in yields (and, as we shall see,
trends in inflation), we have *en passant*, as it were, discussed some of
these movements. For instance, we have referred to the reverse yield
gap and the accompanying inflation trend over our data period and
the impact this appears to have had in influencing the choice (particularly) between fixed interest and equity assets. However, we need to be
more systematic in analysing these trends.

In Figure 5.1 we portray the fixed interest yields (to redemption) of corporate bonds and 'long' government securities and the dividend yield on ordinary shares. What we can note from this figure is that:

1. There is a gap between long gilts and long corporate bonds with the premium being a reward for the default, marketability and after 1969, tax differences. (In 1969, the gains on government bonds were exempt from tax provided the securities were held for one year.) Also we can note, however, that this premium does vary, and quite markedly in some periods, so that at times it may appear profitable to move into corporate bonds at the expense of long gilts.

2. There is a permanent reverse yield gap, i.e. the yields on fixed interest (either gilts or debentures) are always (in our data period at least) in excess of the dividend yield. This gap does vary quite considerably and if we were to examine yield data for earlier periods, we would detect that it took almost 15 years for this trend of a reverse yield gap to appear. Such a trend has been regarded by some (see for example J.L. Carr (24)) as signifying that investors have come to accept that ordinary shares, despite their income variability and price volatility are a better hedge against inflation than fixed interest securities. However, this relationship needs to be subjected to empirical testing, as in some periods equity prices and inflation have been negatively correlated. In consequence we might expect that with an acceleration in the rate of inflation and a shift from fixed interest to ordinary shares, the reverse yield gap would widen. However, as there are a mixture of maturities available in fixed interest securities, particularly in gilts, then will the whole maturity structure of yields follow? The answer to this is illustrated quite simply in Figure 5.2 where we graph short, medium and long gross redemption yields for government securities for the same data period.

The maturity ranges for gilts illustrate that overall, the structure of rates has moved upwards. We can also note several other trends. Up to 1969, the yields are fairly close together, then they diverge markedly, only to come together again in 1973. Thereafter, there are quite wide divergences. An overall cyclical pattern is to be noted and apart from a few quarters in 1964, 1965, 1967 and 1968, the long rate stands above the short. In other words, there is an upward sloping yield curve. The wide divergence noted after 1969 is probably the result of a change in government policy whereby it no longer stood as buyer of the last resort on the long bond market.[1] Without this support, it is not surprising that long rates should rise above the short because substitution may

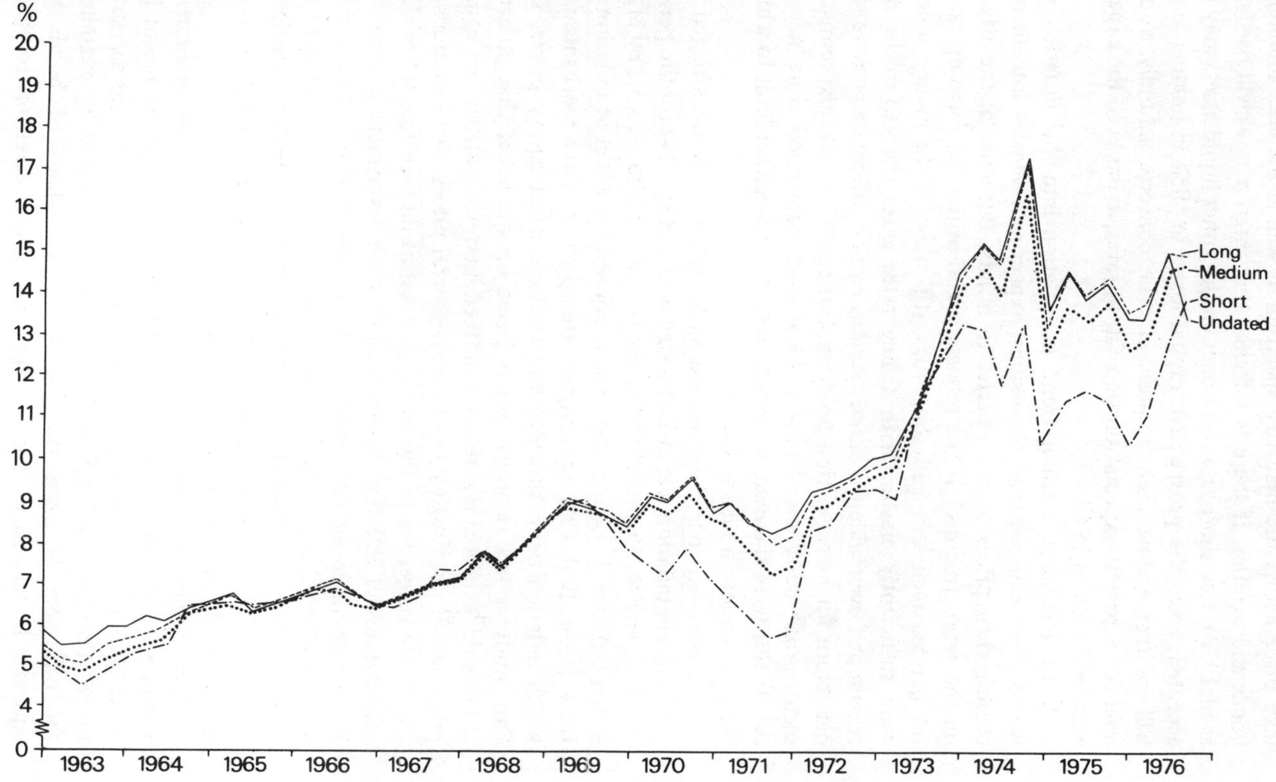

Figure 5.2: Redemption Yields — Government Securities 1963-76

take place across the maturity spectrum as well as between long-term bonds and equities. If there is a feeling that interest rates will rise (say as in 1978), low short rates on bonds and/or other liquid assets may be accepted, since the prospective capital losses implicit in holding longs will militate against their acquisition. The converse naturally would hold for a general expectation of a fall in rates, as has been the experience in the UK in 1977.

If we introduce a rising trend in inflation into this situation we would, from our previous discussions, expect a movement into shares, causing their prices to rise relative to bonds. But what of the effects on the term structure? If the monetary authorities did force up rates, the gap between long and short may still widen if the money supply were sufficiently elastic. With falling rates again the gap might still remain and even widen if *ceteris paribus* equities offered a positive real net return for longer period holdings. For equities to do this, company sector profitability would have to be at least maintained or be increasing. If this were the case, we might expect some market limit to which the yield on long bonds would fall.

The assertion that these various yield differentials are affected by the trends in inflation was in fact tested by J.L. Carr (24) for the period 1960-72, and M. Hughes (86) for the period 1962-76. Studies by M.W. Keran (90) and J. Lintner (98) also examined the effect of inflation on stock prices. Both Carr and Hughes attempted to offer a mechanism by which inflation or inflationary expectations affect equity prices. The Carr study is less rigorous and is based on the belief that inflation reduces the expected real returns on fixed interest securities, but equity prices would rise roughly in line with general prices. The equations he quotes are suggestive of the fact that investors do take account of their expectations of inflation in formulating their investment preferences. We do not quote the Carr results, but we attempted to replicate them on a quarterly basis for the period, 1963-76 for gilts and 1963-75 for corporate bonds. Although we still found the relationship statistically significant, the fit as measured by $\bar{R}^2$ was relatively low and in consequence we do not quote these findings.

The Hughes (86) study represents a more rigorous attempt to evaluate the determinants of the reverse yield gap for the recent UK experience and the related issue that the yield gap may (as suggested by M. Friedman and A.J. Schwartz (63)) be inferred by examining the difference between the current market yields of bonds and equities. In summary form we may quote his regression results as Equation (5.3)

$$(R^L - R^0) = 5.408 + 1.045 \sum_{i=0}^{12} a_i P_{t-i} + 0.013 \sum_{j=0}^{12} b_j G_{t-j}$$
$$ (6.43)$$

$$- 4.422 \, (E/D)_t \qquad\qquad\qquad (5.3)$$
$$ (6.51)$$

where R is the redemption yield on 20-year $R^2 = 0.94$
           government stock
        d is the dividend yield on FT industrial   DW = 1.55
           ordinary share index
        P is the annual rate of change of the Retail
           Price Index
        G is the growth rate of real earnings
        E/D is the ratio of earnings to dividends.

The overall fit of the equation (R^2, the coefficient of determination) is high and the Durbin-Watson statistic (DW) acceptable. The growth of real earnings is perhaps less defendable, but the inflation expectation variable is highly significant and its coefficient of nearly 1.0 would appear to indicate that nominal rates of interest do adjust (in fact over-adjust) to changes in price expectations.

The findings from these two studies would appear to imply that investors can and do in fact assess the relative merits of different assets. The impact of 'inflation' appears to favour equity assets, unless the yield on long (and/or medium) fixed interest (particularly gilts) can exceed that obtainable on short-term assets and equity sufficient to compensate for the vulnerability to capital loss (in both real and nominal terms). As the Carr study only covered the equity yield gap to 1972, it misses the traumatic collapse of stock market prices helped by the existence of dividend and price controls and subsequent rush for liquid assets. The Hughes study, given that it extended to 1976, does cover this and in fact he quotes the fact that the largest errors between actual and estimated bond yields were concentrated in 1974. Certainly we have witnessed in recent years a greater amplitude in the structure of rates with very substantial increases and subsequent falls. In 1977 for example interest was revived in long gilts as a source of potential capital gains with the downward spiral of rates, despite the higher inflation trend.

In Table 5.2 we give the results for corporate bonds, ordinary shares and government securities (including long), where we have incorporated both the supply constraint and the yield gaps between the fixed interest stocks themselves ($R^D - R^L_{t-1}$) and the reverse yield gaps of fixed

Table 5.2 Redemption Yield on Corporate Bonds, Ordinary Shares and Government Securities.

Variables Equation number	Dependent variable	Constant	I_t^C	I_t^O	I_t^G	I_t^{GL}	$(R^D - R_{t-1}^L)$	$(R^D - R_{t-1}^{O1})$	$(R^D - R_{t-1}^{O2})$	$(R^L - R_{t-1}^{O1})$	$\bar{R}^2$	DW	Det. C
5.2 (1)	NA_t^C	27.9* (6.6)	0.31* (0.04)				-14.9* (5.14)				0.68	1.4	0.8
5.2 (2)	NA_t^C	29.5* (6.1)	0.28* (0.04)					-2.9* (0.8)			0.70	1.4	0.72
5.2 (3)	NA_t^C	11.17* (3.2)	0.38* (0.04)						-1.28* (0.57)		0.65	1.3	0.95
5.2 (4)	NA_t^O	-2.8 (8.6)		0.40* (0.07)			7.2* (1.7)				0.56	1.4	1.0
5.2 (5)	NA_t^O	25.1* (6.0)		0.39* (0.08)				3.5* (1.3)			0.46	1.1	1.0
5.2 (6)	NA^G	40.2* (0.02)			0.07* (0.02)		-9.9 (12.4)				0.44	1.6	1.0
5.2 (7)	NA^G	18.1* (9.0)			0.07* (0.01)					3.8 (2.2)	0.47	1.7	0.9
5.2 (8)	NA^{GL}	5.4 (8.8)				0.2* (0.02)	9.7 (8.8)				0.69	1.7	0.9
5.2 (9)	NA^{GL}	16.8* (6.7)				0.2* (0.02)				-0.92 (1.6)	0.69	1.7	0.9

Glossary:

NA^C net acquisitions of corporate bonds
NA^G net acquisitions of government securities
I^G issues of corporate bonds
I^{GL} issues of government securities
R^D yield on corporate bonds
R^{O2} earnings yield

NA^O net acquisitions of ordinary shares
NA^{GL} net acquisitions of over 15 years to maturity government securities
I^O issues of ordinary shares
I^{GL} issues over 15 years to maturity government securities
R^{O1} dividend yield
R^L yield on long government securities (over 15 years to maturity)

interest (corporate and government bonds) and ordinary shares. We use two measures here of the yield on ordinary shares: dividend yield as in Figure 5.1 and earnings yield. Both yields have their relative attractions as dividend yield gives a measure of the distributed income in respect of the current price of the index of shares (in this case the actuaries industrial 500 shares), whereas the earnings yield is more of a longer-term measure on the overall earning prospects of the firm. We are assuming that these yields are independent of the actions of life offices, though this is more suspect in the case of debentures than the other two markets.

If we take the corporate bond equations first (Equations 5.2 (1) to 5.2 (3)) then what we note overall is that the $\bar{R}^2$ are quite high. Focussing on the yield gap with government bonds ($R^D - R^L_{t-1}$) a negative sign is recorded, but the coefficient is statistically significant at the 5 per cent level. This is perhaps a surprising result since as we regard gilts and debentures as substitutes (see Chapter 2), we would *ceteris paribus* expect the demand for debentures to be linked with a widening of the yield gap[2] as debentures only appear attractive if there is a sufficient margin to compensate for the added risk. In the government bond equation the same coefficient is again negative, the sign we could reasonably expect *a priori*, but it is not significant. In the long bond equation, it returns to a positive sign. The reverse yield gaps[3] are significant in most equations and in the corporate bond equation, the coefficients are correctly signed, if we presume a narrowing of the gap would favour fixed interest. But this is not borne out in the gilts Equation (5.2 (7)) though it is if long gilts are taken (Equation 5.2 (9)). For the ordinary share equations, the reverse yield gap coefficients are correctly signed and significant.

Having examined those four factors which would appear to be important in actually influencing the strategic investment decision, we are left with the question of the availability of funds (or what we may refer to as the income constraint) and the existing stock position. We can use various income measures here. One possibility is to use the net addition to policy reserves which represents the new money available for investment. This does have certain problems associated with it, in that the data are available only annually, so interpolation is required without any satisfactory measures available for this. In addition such data preclude the availability of funds from other parts of the portfolio, though this can in part be handled by including short-term assets which we have argued may act as a convenient buffer. We would expect from the inclusion of these that the coefficients would be positive for $t-1$ and negative for t. The main income variable is to use total net acquisitions. This includes both the net new funds available for investment *and* those which are released from existing investment in the portfolio and involve a change in the stock positions. *A priori*, we would of course expect a positive sign on this, unless the asset in question features negative net acquisitions over a large part of the period. Recall that in the Ryan study we indicated some surprise at the positive sign on the preference share and local authority securities equations as these recorded negative net acquisitions over a large part of our data period, particularly up to 1972. If the investment process is sequential (a la Munro), with the balance sheet segmented, then of course the income constraint has to be adjusted for the prior allocations.

We are now in a position to turn to specifying individual demand equations for the six asset classes already delineated at the start of this section and this we do in Section 5.3.

5.3 Individual Demand Specifications

In this section we wish to capture as much of the actual variables which appear to shape the net acquisitions. We are aware that in most econometric work it is almost impossible to explain the events as they really are, in that the data limitations and the time period (in our case a quarter) on which data are available often militate against this; irrespective of the arguments used in the equations. We commence with corporate bonds or debentures as they are more often termed in the UK.

Corporate Bonds

We can recall that in Table 5.2 we obtained quite a good relationship with the issues data and either of the yield gaps. We did attempt further analysis here utilising various lag schemes to represent expected interest rates, but these versions produced little difference in fit or coefficients from those assuming 'static expectations'. We also used price indices (logged) on the basis that securities are traded in price rather than yield, but the results were not materially different; so we do not quote these findings.

We tried many different equations incorporating the various changes in liability structure (linear interpolation was used to derive the quarterly series, though we recognised this as a questionable practice), and these results were generally perverse, as were the income constraints attempted; policy reserves, total net acquisitions and the latter adjusted for prior allocation of other assets. We also tested for the hypothesis that shorter-term assets are used as a buffer, built up and subsequently run down to accommodate net acquisitions. This formulation was tried, as was the use of an adjusted data series where an estimate of the short-term assets required for transactions purposes was applied to the data to derive a series of assets held for portfolio purposes. Neither formulation was statistically significant, though the coefficients supported the buffer hypothesis. We do not quote these results. The incorporation of a lagged dependent variable also did not improve the fit of the equation. What was significant, however, was the inclusion of a dummy variable, D(2) to pick up the twin influences in 1969 of the freeing of capital gains on gilts and the change in official support of the long gilt market. We tried dummies for three quarters in 1969, and finally adopted the second quarter one as this combined, in terms of announcement time, the two influences. An examination of Table 5.3 indicates the fact that this coefficient is highly statistically significant in all four equations presented. We also utilised the issues of ordinary shares (I_t^O), (Equation 5.3 (3) and 5.3 (4)) and the positive sign on the coefficient indicates complementarity, whereas the negative sign on the issues of government securities (I_t^G) goes some way to confirming substitutability. These four equations represent the 'best' set of results obtained and whilst the fit is good, they leave a lot to be desired; for instance we do not have an income constraint present. It would appear though that in periods when issues are made, funds are made available for investment in debentures.

Ordinary Shares

The relationship obtained in Table 5.2, where we combined yield gaps and the issues of ordinary shares, was only moderately successful. As with corporate bonds, we did attempt to specify more rigorously expected yields without any success. Our equations where we included the inter-relationship of assets and liabilities were more successful and we quote two examples of these as Equations (5.4 (1) and 5.4 (2)) where we have included (after 1970) linked policies (ΔLP) and pension provisions (ΔPP) lagged one period. The justification for the lag is that whilst the inflow is throughout the quarter, unless we specify a series of expected inflows, investment managers do not have full information on the availability of funds from the start of period t, until the end of $t-1$. Both coefficients are correctly signed and significant at the 5 per cent level. This is to be expected as many linked policies are directly related to ordinary shares, whereas the increase in pension business will, with the continuing inflation, force investment managers

Table 5.3: Corporate Bonds (Debentures) Asset Demand Equations 1963 (1) – 1974 (4)

Variables / Equation number	Dependent variable	Constant	I_t^C	$(R^D-R^L)_{t-1}$	$(R^D-R^{01})_{t-1}$	I_t^O	I_t^G	NA_{t-1}^C	D(2)	$\bar{R}^2$	DW	Det. C
5.3 (1)	NA_t^C	25.2* (6.5)	0.25* (0.04)	-3.2 (5.3)	1.7 (1.4)				-25.3* (6.8)	0.77	1.9	0.08
5.3 (2)	NA_t^C	29.1* (5.6)	0.26* (0.04)	-2.9 (5.3)			-0.005 (0.004)		-16.5* (5.0)	0.77	1.9	0.1
5.3 (3)	NA_t^C	24.6* (5.5)	0.24* (0.04)	0.4 (5.0)		0.07* (0.02)			-21.1* (4.2)	0.80	2.0	0.1
5.3 (4)	NA_t^C	27.3* (6.8)	0.25* (0.04)	0.12 (5.20)		0.08* (0.03)		-0.08 (0.1)	-22.6* (4.7)	0.80	1.9	0.2

Notes as for Table 5.2 except D (2) – shift dummy.

Table 5.4: Ordinary Shares — Asset Demand Equations 1963 (1) – 1974 (4)

Variables	Dependent variable	Constant	I_t^0	ΔLP_{t-1}	ΔPP_{t-1}	$(R^L - R^{01})_{t-1}$	TNA_t	STA_t	TNA^{AA1}	NA_{t-1}^0	$\bar{R}^2$	DW	Det. C
Equation number													
5.4 (1)	NA_t^0	18.3* (5.9)	0.39* (0.07)	0.3* (0.08)							0.52	1.3	1.0
5.4 (2)	NA_t^0	7.6 (7.7)	0.42* (0.07)		0.09* (0.03)						0.51	1.3	1.0
5.4 (3)	NA_t^0	−23.0* (12.0)	0.26* (0.07)				0.25* (0.06)				0.57	1.5	0.9
5.4 (4)	NA_t^0	−2.8 (8.6)	0.41* (0.07)			7.1* (1.6)		−0.12* (0.06)			0.56	1.3	0.9
5.4 (5)	NA_t^0	−25.8* (11.9)	0.35* (0.07)			4.1* (1.7)			0.22* (0.08)		0.60	1.7	0.7
5.4 (6)	NA_t^0	−0.05 (7.6)	0.27* (0.07)			0.7 (2.1)			0.17* (0.08)	0.29* (0.12)	0.66	2.3	0.3

ΔLP new linked policies
ΔPP new pension provisions
TNA AA1 total net acquisitions adjusted for prior net acquisitions of loans and mortgages, debentures and property
STA net acquisitions of short-term assets

to seek the potentially higher returns (particularly capital growth) that ordinary shares can give. Whilst these results are encouraging, if both types of new business are included in the same equation (which we do not quote), then neither are significant and the sign on the pension provisions coefficient becomes perverse. A worrying feature indeed.

We tried the various measures of the overall income constraints and apart from the change in total policy reserves (and even here the coefficient was positively signed), the coefficients were significant and correctly signed. We quote the results for total net acquisitions (TNA), short-term assets (STA) and the adjusted total net acquisitions which has allowed for the prior allocation of funds to loans and mortgages, debentures and property (TNA^{AA1}). These are given as Equations 5.4 (3) to 5.4 (5). We tried many other specifications, including the various issues of marketable securities, without any material success. The link with the stock position via the lagged dependent variable did produce a significant coefficient with a speed of adjustment broadly in line with that obtained by Ryan. This is illustrated in the final equation given (Equation 5.4 (6)). In this equation we have dropped the liability structure links of ΔLP and ΔPP in favour of including a total net acquisitions variable (to include both would cause some double counting) which allows for the segmenting of the portfolio we have stressed previously. The fit of 0.66 is obstinately low and whilst it does compare favourably with that obtained by Ryan, a direct comparison with the Munro model is not possible. By including the lagged dependent variable, it produces the insignificant coefficients on the yield gap term $(R^D - R^{01})_{t-1}$ and the adjusted income term (TNA^{AA1}).

Government Securities

The equations presented in Table 5.2 indicated a relatively low fit for the government bonds. Yet this is a major asset in holdings and as we indicated in Chapter 2, gilt-edged securities act as the 'model' by which to compare other assets. Whilst we have suggested that gilts can act as a complementary set of assets for holdings of ordinary shares and property, there are occasions when it would appear, from the net acquisitions data discussed in Chapter 2, that they are being utilised as a strategic liquid reserve (see G.T. Pepper (120) for further support to this argument) and run down when more profitable (in terms of yield), opportunities arise in other markets. As with corporate bonds and ordinary shares, we were unable to generate expectations series of yields which produced any material differences in the equations, so we are forced back to 'static expectations'. This is perhaps surprising given

Table 5.5: Government Securities — Asset Demand Equations 1963 (1) — 1974 (4)

Variables	Dependent variable	Constant	I_t^G	$(R^D-R^L)_{t-1}$	$(R^L-R^{01})_{t-1}$	STA_t	STA_{t-1}	$D(2)$	NA_{t-1}^G	$\bar{R}^2$	DW	Det. C
Equation number												
5.5 (1)	NA_t^G	15.9* (7.4)	0.05* (0.001)		6.4* (1.8)	−0.31* (0.07)				0.64	1.4	0.8
5.5 (2)	NA_t^G	19.3* (8.7)	0.07* (0.01)		2.9 (2.1)		0.21* (0.10)			0.50	1.3	0.9
5.5 (3)	NA_t^G	17.2 (9.3)	0.07* (0.01)		3.4 (2.4)				0.06 (0.13)	0.46	1.8	0.8
5.5 (4)	NA_t^G	22.2* (9.7)	0.04* (0.01)		0.9 (3.3)	−0.35* (0.07)		28.5 (16.8)		0.65	1.3	0.8
5.5 (5)	NA_t^{GL}	16.4* (6.8)	0.21* (0.02)		−1.3 (1.6)	0.06 (0.06)				0.69	1.8	0.8
5.5 (6)	NA_t^{GL}	−1.0 (9.1)	0.21* (0.02)	24.6* (11.3)				−18.4* (9.2)		0.71	1.9	0.5

the relative success of the Munro use of an extrapolative mechanism that we discussed in Chapter 4.

In Table 5.5 we summarise some of the results that we found using the schema adopted for the other two marketable asset types. Once again, although we used various measures of policy types, the results were inconclusive, so are not quoted. Additionally, the only overall income variable that was statistically significant was short-term assets (Equations 5.5 (1) and 5.5 (2)). We tried a lagged dependent variable but this was not significant (Equation 5.5 (3)) neither were the inclusion of the issues of the other marketable securities (we do not quote these results). Where we included the same shift dummy (D(2)) of the corporate bond equations, there was no material difference in fit, and the yield gap coefficient was no longer significant (Equation 5.5 (4)). In conclusion then the overall fit remains obstinately low. This is, however, better than that achieved by both Ryan and Munro.

By disaggregating the gilts into the various maturity ranges, the only meaningful results we could obtain were those for longs (over 15 years to maturity). Since these dominate the portfolio both in holdings and net acquisitions, the inability to model net acquisitions of shorts (0–5 years to maturity), medium (5–15 years to maturity) and undated is perhaps not so important. However, it does mean that we cannot explain the switching between the maturity ranges which may occur. (See A.T. Grant (70), G.T. Pepper (120) and J.B. Marshall (103) for a discussion of switching in gilt-edged securities.) For the net acquisitions of long bonds (NA^{GL}) the short-term asset coefficients were no longer significant so we only quote the use of one of these in Equation (5.5 (5)). The best equation we obtained was Equation 5.5 (6) where we included the shift dummy D(2) and the yield gap with corporate bonds. This gave a good fit of 71 per cent with the three regression coefficients significant at the 5 per cent level. This is certainly a better result than that which we achieved for a model of the net acquisitions of the whole gilt-edged maturity range.

Loans and Mortgages

Loans and mortgages are assets which are expressed in nominal values with, as we have seen, no recognised secondary market. We note from Chapter 2 that for the overall position the portfolio proportion remained relatively constant at 17 per cent up to 1970, thereafter it has fallen to 12 per cent in 1976. In net acquisitions the proportion has fluctuated considerably from −2 per cent in 1976 to 28 per cent in 1965.

To obtain a better picture of the possible causes of such movements we need to divide the asset group into the two subsets recognised in the published data, namely house purchase loans and other loans and mortgages (including overseas). We consider house purchase loans first.

House Purchase Loans

We cannot advance any particular liability structure that is determined or best suited by the attributes of house mortgages. That is not to say that they are not a choice asset *per se*, but given what we have said about their use in increasing overall business, particularly endowment (with profits) and giving diversification, then these are non-yield attributes which we cannot model. Additionally we have argued previously that life companies are not active participants in housing finance and, indeed, life offices are only on the periphery of this particular market, as we illustrated in Chapter 2. But up to 1974 they have remained net lenders. Although life offices act in a more passive role in granting house mortgages, making the own yield term of lesser importance. Nevertheless, we should attempt to develop a demand equation for mortgages if only to give some predictions as to what factors may cause the demand. We can hypothesise several factors that may be important in this process. In the first instance, we might expect that a credit rationing situation would force borrowers to life offices to seek a mortgage as an alternative source; and one suitable proxy here would be to utilise the liquidity ratio of building societies. Building societies tend to build up their liquidity in some periods, causing a mortgage famine, and in others to run it down. We can recall that we discussed the use of this variable in Chapter 4 in the Munro model. There we argued for the overspill hypothesis that we would expect a negative sign on the coefficient. Whilst this excess demand, even in a period of relative mortgage plenty, may be an important factor in generating demand for mortgages from life offices, the life offices do have the right to refuse to lend, so that we need to consider other criteria too. These would include the sort of influences discussed in the case of the other assets examined so far.

In Table 5.6 we present a series of results (Equations 5.6 (1) to (3)) which test the above factors and also posit a stock adjustment mechanism which is significant with a relatively low speed of adjustment, which is what we would expect *a priori*. The spillover hypothesis finds support both in terms of the negative sign on the coefficient on building society liquidity (*BSLiq*) and the positive sign on the house price index (*HPI*). Whilst the fit achieved on Equation 5.6 (3) is very encouraging, we could not find any link with the various income constraints, so as to

Table 5.6: Loans and Mortgages — Asset Demand Equations 1963 (1) — 1974 (4)

Variables	Dependent variable	Constant	R^M	HPI	$BSLiq_{t-1}$	TNA	Lag of dependent variable	$\bar{R}^2$	DW	Det. C
Equation number										
5.6 (1)	NA^H	76.1* (13.5)	2.8* (0.7)		−5.2* (0.77)			0.55	1.0	1.0
5.6 (2)	NA^H	78.0* (16.0)	2.5 (1.7)	0.007 (0.03)	−5.2* (0.8)			0.54	1.0	1.0
5.6 (3)	NA^H	47.4* (10.9)		0.03* (0.009)	−2.8* (0.6)		0.60* (0.09)	0.78	1.9	0.7
5.6 (4)	NA^{OL}	9.6* (4.7)				−0.006 (0.02)	0.58* (0.13)	0.27	1.9	1.0
5.6 (5)	NA^{LM}	94.6* (27.8)			−5.2* (1.6)	0.04* (0.02)	0.51* (0.12)	0.65	2.2	1.0

NA^H net acquisitions of house purchase loans
NA^{OL} net acquisitions of other loans and mortgages
HPI house price index
BSLiq building society liquidity ratio
TNA total net acquisitions of assets
R^M rate of interest on mortgages

improve the equation, so we do not quote these results.

Turning to other loans and mortgages, with the removal of house purchase loans, we are left with a rather amorphous grouping for which it is virtually impossible to determine a yield term and difficult to focus attention on any market consideration which might be relevant. In consequence, all that we can realistically utilise is a simple stock adjustment framework and attempt to identify some form of income constraint. We quote only that result which includes a lagged dependent variable Equation (5.6 (4)). The equation does indicate statistical significance on the stock term, but the overall fit is low and the implied speed of adjustment is of similar magnitude to that for house purchase loans. We could find no fit using the various income terms tried in other specifications. With such a relatively low fit, we decided to re-estimate the equations by attempting to model for all loans and mortgages, since the only other alternative would be to relegate these other loans and mortgages to the residual asset class.

Total Loans and Mortgages

We tried several specifications here including using the yield gaps we have utilised in our asset groupings. What we find in Equation 5.6 (5) is that the stock adjustment term is significant and that the building society liquid asset ratio in $t-1$ remains significant and correctly signed. The inclusion of an income constraint (TNA) also produces a significant coefficient. Overall the fit is quite respectable.

Land, Property and Ground Rents

As with the previous asset grouping, this asset class is an amalgam of various investments which extend to agricultural holdings, city centre property and land held freehold and leasehold. Our discussions in Chapter 2 revealed that some of these holdings could properly be regarded as 'equity' investment whilst others, particularly the ground rent element were a 'fixed interest' type investment. In addition we indicated that the growth of linked policies, some of which were linked to a 'property' fund, provided a possible element determining the funds available for investment. Certainly, as these policies are sold on the basis of giving a hedge against inflation, and as our discussions with life managers themselves have confirmed that the 'equity' element is the dominant one in the asset grouping, then this how we will judge it for the purposes of the study.

One of the main difficulties in attempting to model the net acquisition of 'property' is the absence of any clear yield term. This prompted

Munro, for example, to treat the property acquisitions as predetermined. But Ryan did use a yield term, though he did not reveal his sources. We know, however, that property values are subject to swings, similar, though not as marked or as frequent, to those experienced by the stock market, and although there is no recognised secondary market, trading does occur as was illustrated in Table 2.16. In deciding how to approach this yield question we considered the utilisation of a price index which could reflect the property values, in similar vein to the price indices available for ordinary shares and fixed interest stocks. The problem here is that no comparable published index is available and we have to look for a proxy. One suggestion that we explored was to use an index which reflects house prices. Not that life offices are significant buyers of private houses, but this index may serve as a convenient catch-all yield variable. In the equations we present in this section we find that this yield term does perform particularly well, probably due to the time trend in that net acquisitions were, on the overall, upward, and so too was the index. We did, however, try other proxies, but we finally concluded that on balance we should use the house price index. We do stress, however, that we recognise the charges that could be levelled against us in following such an approach.

In Table 5.7 we present the best results we obtained following the criteria adopted for all the other asset classes discussed so far. These illustrate that the fit is extremely good, though the Durbin-Watson statistic in Equation 5.7 (3) does indicate auto-correlation. Where the lagged dependent variable is included the fit increases and the own yield (HPI) appears to perform well but not the reverse yield gap, though this is expressed in price indices. The inclusion of the rate on short-term assets (R^{STA}) also produces a significant coefficient. The sign, however, is more difficult to explain since we would expect property investment to fall during periods of high short rates, as the latter are normally reflective of tight business conditions.

The yield gap with ordinary shares is also significant and positively signed. The rationalisation for this is that ordinary shares and property can be substitutes within the portfolio. One other hypothesis which we tested for was the sequential nature of the allocation process. Our feelings were that it was not *the* primary choice asset that Munro argued for and we tested several hypotheses here including the use of the issues of other marketable securities. The only adjusted income series significant and correctly signed was that for TNA^A, total net acquisitions adjusted for the prior net acquisitions of loans and mortgages (Equation 5.7 (3)).

Table 5.7: Land, Property and Ground Rents — Asset Demand Equations 1963 (1) — 1974 (4)

Variables	Dependent variable	Constant	HPI_{t-1}	$(R_p^L - R_p^0)_{t-1}$	$(HPI - R_p^0)_{t-1}$	R_{t-1}^{STA}	TNA^A	NA_{t-1}^P	$\bar{R}^2$	DW	Det. C
Equation number											
5.7 (1)	NA^P	−4.98 (4.7)	0.20* (0.05)	0.06 (0.05)				0.47* (0.13)	0.85	2.2	0.2
5.7 (2)	NA^P	14.4* (5.9)	0.14* (0.05)	0.04 (0.04)		2.9* (1.2)		0.42* (0.12)	0.86	2.4	0.05
5.7 (3)	NA^P	19.9* (5.2)			0.24* (0.03)		0.07* (0.03)		0.78	1.1	0.4

NA^P net acquisitions of property

R^{STA} yield on short term assets

R_p^L price index for government long bonds

R_p^0 price index for ordinary shares

TNA^A total net acquisitions adjusted for prior acquisitions of loans and mortgages

Short-term Assets

We have already referred to the liquidity needs of life offices. The amount of liquidity which is required for transactions purposes to provide the necessary working capital for normal life business will be related in some way to the business in force and the new business written. Indeed, we can refer to the adjustment we made in the short-term assets to take account of this in our specification of the other assets classes; though in the event, these adjusted data (with the transactions element removed) produced no material difference in the equations, when used in place of the unadjusted. The primary liquidity requirements have arisen, however, from the needs of portfolio management to shift the portfolio from one area of investment to another. These shifts would appear (from the data we analysed in Chapter 2) to have occurred to obtain investments which at the particular time seem to provide the best solution to the investment problem. The investment environment facing the life offices is continually changing, though these changes do not follow any regular or systematic fashion. In consequence, short-term assets are used (as we have already argued) as a buffer to be built up in periods when available alternatives are limited and subsequently run down when opportunities arise and/or when uncertainties (e.g. 1974/5) subside. They are thus a convenient way of remaining fully invested, yet giving the manoeuvrability required if the composition of the portfolio is to be changed later. This can be achieved without incurring a capital loss on securities sold. There is thus no 'locking in' effect that would happen with longer-term assets. However, in holding them, life offices do face the risk of being caught too short.

These portfolio needs are likely to dominate the liquidity holdings (and net acquisitions) as the liquidity preference needs for actual transaction purposes can be anticipated with a fair degree of accuracy. In consequence the extreme (and increasing) variations need to be modelled from the point of view of the portfolio of assets, rather than the portfolio of liabilities. If we only had to model the transactions demand rather than the 'excess' liquidity, we would argue for a partial stock adjustment model on the basis that there may be some element of forecasting error giving rise to the less than instantaneous adjustment to the desired relationship. To accommodate the excess liquidity, such a relationship is more tenuous. Clearly holdings will need to increase by virtue of the overall increase in total assets, since the ability to make any significant shift in the portfolio will be affected by its overall size. Therefore a partial stock adjustment model may be in order. Additionally, we have to take into account the opportunity cost to the life fund of the next best alternative to short-term assets, having due regard to these factors. This could be any one of the other asset groups to which we have referred.

As short-term assets do have a recognisable yield and as at times this may be quite high, then we need to include an own yield (R^{STA}). We tried several and we finally selected minimum lending rate as being a useful proxy. To test for substitution with the other assets we tried two methods. The first was to use issues data for other assets. When these are low (often in periods of uncertainty), then unless there are favourable opportunities in loans, mortgages and property, liquid assets will be built up. We might therefore expect the total issues of marketable securities (ΣI_t) to be a significant variable (with a negative sign). If we can deduce that property will also more than likely follow the same pattern as these marketable securities, then we may be able to account for all of the substitutability in this one term. The second method was to test for substitution effects more directly by concentrating on the movements of yield gaps, particularly the reverse yield gap ($R^L - R^{01}$) and term structure yield gap ($R^L - R^S$).

In Table 5.8 we quote some of the formulations we tried and we can note that the ΣI_t term and own yield are significant (at the 5 per cent level) and correctly signed in all equations. In addition, both the yield gaps are significant, although the lagged dependent variable coefficient was not significant in any of the formulations used. We did try other formulations which tested directly for the expectations of inflation, but we could not improve on the relationships quoted in Table 5.8. Even adjusting the series to take out the transactions element did not produce results basically different from those referred to earlier, so we do not quote these findings. Any attempt to disaggregate the asset group to model separate demand equations for the constituent parts met with very low overall fits, despite numerous specifications. Overall, therefore, we have a disappointing set of results for short-term assets.

Residual Assets

The residual assets comprise of preference shares, overseas government securities, other overseas assets, agents' balances and other unspecified assets. This is too heterogeneous a group to attempt any meaningful analysis. Our previous discussions have implicitly covered some of the factors likely to affect these particular residual assets. In the case of overseas assets we have argued that these may be held for two reasons. In the first place they can 'match' the premium income

Table 5.8: Short-term Assets — Asset Demand Equations 1963 (1) – 1974 (4)

Variables / Equation number	Dependent variable	Constant	R^{STA}_{t-1}	$(R^L - R^S)_{t-1}$	$(R^L - R^{01})_{t-1}$	ΣI_t	NA^{STA}_{t-1}	$\bar{R}^2$	DW	Det. C
5.8 (1)	NA^{STA}_t	−69.9* (25.8)	12.0* (3.4)	29.1* (8.8)		−0.07* (0.02)		0.40	2.1	1.0
5.8 (2)	NA^{STA}_t	−79.2* (27.9)	13.7* (3.6)		28.2* (10.3)	−0.08* (0.02)		0.36	2.1	0.9
5.8 (3)	NA^{STA}_t	−84.3* (28.3)	14.6* (3.7)		29.2* (10.3)	−0.08* (0.02)	−0.2 (0.2)	0.36	1.9	0.9
5.8 (4)	NA^{STA}_t	−76.2* (26.0)	13.0* (3.5)	31.0* (8.9)		−0.07* (0.02)	−0.2 (0.2)	0.41	1.8	0.9

NA^{STA} net acquisitions of short-term assets

R^L yield on long government bonds (over 15 years)

R^S yield on short government bonds (up to 5 years)

R^{01} dividend yield on ordinary shares

ΣI_t total issues of marketable securities

R^{STA} yield on short-term assets

derived from overseas thus reducing the uncertainty of exchange rate depreciation of the £ sterling. Additionally they can be held to improve the overall yield, in that the earning power of some of these assets may be in excess of other yields currently available in the UK. In this study, we are not in a position to prosecute these lines of argument any further. For preference shares these have declined in market significance with the growth of issues of corporate bonds and indeed over most of our data period, life companies have simply run their holdings down (mainly via redemptions) as the data in Chapter 2 revealed. Whilst we did attempt to model this, our results are not worth quoting.

Notes

1. Previously the Bank of England always stood ready to deal in Treasury Bills and gilt-edged stocks at a price so as to maintain a stable and effective market so that holders could switch in and out at will. In May 1969 however, the Bank announced that the official buying price for stocks within three months maturity would not be tied to Treasury Bill rate but that the government broker still stood ready to receive offers of such stock. Then in July it was announced that the authorities would no longer announce the price at which they were prepared to sell tap stocks, but would instead consider the bids made by the market. In part these actions may have caused some of the revealed rate structure on the market so that the dummy may be picking up this aspect as well.

2. In 1969 the capital gain on gilts was exempt from tax provided the securities were held for one year. This did not apply to debentures so this is another variable which would influence the choice between the two assets.

3. We quote results for both variants of the fixed interest element and two measures of the yield on ordinary shares for the gap with debentures but only one measure, dividend yield for gilts. The inclusion of the earnings yield makes no material difference.

6.1 Introduction

In this chapter we wish to try to bring together our findings from Chapter 5 into a more coherent framework. We can recall that we specified individual demand equations for six asset groupings *as if* they were separate decisions. Whilst we were in effect also indicating the interdependence among these assets either directly (use of yield gaps, issues data, adjusted income series) or indirectly (by recognising that the assets possessed different characteristics essential to the portfolio), we did not at that stage attempt to formalise those equations into a comprehensive model. Nor did we attempt to use our demand equations to test for their predictive power outside of the sample period. The purpose of this chapter is to take up these two points. In Section 6.2 we indicate the predictive power of the summary equations from Chapter 5 for the period 1975-6 (eight quarters), as well as giving the overall results for the extended sample period. In Section 6.3 we indicate the problems of attempting to combine these equations into an overall model and we give a summary of our 'best' attempts. We again test for its predictive power, and then we re-estimate the whole model for the extended data series 1963-76.

6.2 The Predictive Power of the Individual Demand Specifications

In this section we measure the predictive power of the various demand equations we specified in Chapter 5. We do not actually forecast these future demands as this would require us to forecast values of net new funds and the like. We recognise, however, that such *ex ante* forecasts are necessary and this is a line of work which we will follow up in a future study. For our present purposes we use *ex post* forecasts, that is we test the ability of the models to predict the actual values of dependent variables *given* the actual values of independent variables. In predicting outside of the sample period we need to stress the difficulties and dangers involved in this process. The actual values we attempt to predict are for the period 1975 (1) to 1976 (4) inclusive and we are in effect assuming that the 'structure' of the asset demand equations for the period 1963-74 holds also for 1975-6. Yet we know that the events in the financial markets of these two years (and 1974 for that matter) were quite traumatic. We can cite several instances, some of which are interconnected. To be specific, the collapse of the property boom, the collapse of stock market prices, record levels of interest rates and levels of inflation, the failure of the secondary bank structure and some small life insurance companies, all contributed to produce great uncertainty and a lack of confidence in the future. We have seen that the end result of this was the movement into cash and short-term assets. It is for this abnormal period that we are using our models to predict *ex post*. We are therefore arguing that *a priori* we might not be able to predict particularly well. To test the predictive power of the demand equations, we use a fairly standard measure, namely H. Theil's inequality coefficient, U (160). This tests the ability of a model to predict changes in variables as well as giving us a ready comparison with the predictive power of the naive, zero change extrapolative model of the dependent variable (that is where $NA_{t+1} = NA_t$). The size of the inequality coefficient, U, may of course vary between zero and infinity where a value of zero implies perfect prediction (predicted equal actual values); a value of one implies that the model is no better than zero change extrapolation; and any value greater than one implies that the predictive performance of the model is inferior to that of zero change extrapolation.

The computational formula for U is

$$U = [\{ \sum_{i=1}^{n} (P_i - A_i)^2 \}/\{ \sum_{i=1}^{n} A_i^2 \}] \tag{6.1}$$

where P is the predicted value of the dependent variable and A is the actual value of this variable. Whilst we are predicting over a reasonable time period, it may still be the case that one large error may bias the value of U; which may be less affected by a larger sample of predictions (say four years) if these errors are normally distributed with zero mean. However, even if we had used a larger sample and thus had removed any bias, the predictive performance of the models over the period may still appear poor if the variance of the predicted and actual values is substantially different or if the actual and predicted values are poorly correlated (see Theil (160) Chapter 2).

In Table 6.1 we take the summary equations for the period 1963-74 from Chapter 5 and for the sake of convenience, for our present purposes, we repeat them here, though we re-number them to accord with the numbering of this chapter.[1] In Table 6.2 we then give the Theil inequality coefficients for these equations.

The first impression to be gained overall from this table is that the

Table 6.1: Summary Equations for Individual Demand Specifications, 1963-74

Equation number	6.1 (1)	6.1 (2)	6.1 (3)	6.1 (4)	6.1 (5)	6.1 (6)	6.1 (7)	6.1 (8)	6.1 (9)	6.1 (10)	6.1 (11)	6.1 (12)	6.1 (13)	6.1 (14)
Variables														
Dependent variable	NA^C	NA^C	NA^C	NA^O	NA^G	NA^{GL}	NA^{GL}	NA^{LM}	NA^{OL}	NA^H	NA^P	NA^P	NA^{STA}	NA^{STA}
Constant	29.1* (5.6)	24.6* (5.6)	27.3* (6.8)	-0.05 (7.6)	15.9* (7.4)	16.4* (6.8)	-1.0 (9.1)	94.6* (27.8)	9.6* (4.7)	47.4* (10.9)	14.4* (5.9)	-4.98 (4.7)	-84.3* (28.3)	-76.2* (26.0)
I_t^C	0.26* (0.04)	0.24* (0.04)	0.25* (0.04)											
O_t		0.07* (0.02)	0.08* (0.03)	0.27* (0.07)										
G_t	-0.005 (0.004)				0.05* (0.001)									
I_t^{GL}						0.2* (0.02)	0.2* (0.02)							
$(R^D-R^{01})_{t-1}$				0.7 (2.1)										
$(R^D-R^L)_{t-1}$	-2.9 (5.3)	0.4 (5.0)	0.12 (5.2)											
$(R^L-R^{01})_{t-1}$					6.4* (1.8)	-1.3 (1.6)	24.6* (11.3)							
$(R^L-R^S)_{t-1}$													29.2* (10.3)	31.0* (8.9)
$BSLiq_{t-1}$								-5.2* (1.6)		-2.8* (0.6)				

	(1)	(2)	(3)	(4)	(5)	(6)	(7)	(8)	(9)	(10)	(11)	(12)	(13)	(14)
TNA								0.04* (0.02)	−0.006 (0.02)					
TNA^{AA1}				0.17* (0.08)										
STA					−0.31* (0.07)	0.06 (0.06)								
R_{t-1}^{STA}										2.9* (1.2)			14.6* (3.7)	13.0* (3.5)
HPI										0.03* (0.01)				
HPI_{t-1}											0.14* (0.05)	0.2* (0.05)		
$(R_p^L - R_p^O)_{t-1}$											0.04 (0.04)	0.06 (0.05)		
ΣI_t													−0.08* (0.02)	−0.07* (0.02)
D(2)	−16.5* (5.0)	−21.1* (4.2)	−22.6* (4.7)				−18.4* (9.2)							
Lag of dependent variable			−0.08 (0.1)	0.29* (0.12)				0.51* (0.12)	0.58* (0.13)	0.60* (0.09)	0.42* (0.12)	0.47* (0.13)	−0.2 (0.2)	−0.2 (0.2)
$\bar{R}^2$	0.77	0.80	0.80	0.66	0.64	0.69	0.71	0.65	0.27	0.78	0.86	0.85	0.36	0.41
DW	1.9	2.0	1.9	2.3	1.4	1.8	1.9	2.2	1.9	1.9	2.4	2.2	1.9	1.8
Det. C	0.08	0.1	0.2	0.3	0.8	0.8	0.5	1.0	1.0	0.7	0.05	0.2	0.9	0.9

Table 6.2: Predictive Performance of Individual Asset Demand
Specification 1975 (1) — 1976 (4)

Models	1	2	3
Variables predicted			
Debentures			
(Equations 6.1 (1) to (3))	0.5326	0.6347	0.6344
Ordinary shares (6.1 (4))	0.4793		
Government securities:[a]			
Total (6.1 (5))	0.9121		
Longs (6.1 (6) to (7))	0.2227	0.4582	
Loans and mortgages:			
Total (6.1 (8))	0.5710		
Others (6.1 (9))	0.5302		
House purchase loans (6.1 (10))	0.1977		
Property (6.1 (11) to (12))	0.1062	0.1399	
Short-term assets (6.1 (13) to (14))	0.8089	0.9292	

All elements are values of U.

a. Where we utilised this equation was with a lagged dependent variable although the fit was inferior, the value for U was 0.2346. Similarly for long bonds the value of U was 0.2066 and 0.2735 respectively.

equations do very well with all the Us being less than one. Within this range of 0 to 1 the performances do range from relatively poor to very good, but certainly these sorts of values do give us positive encouragement. Whilst this table should be relatively self-explanatory (given what we have said already), we can focus on some particularly good results. These were found in the case of property and house purchase loans. For government securities (including one formulation for long bonds) the values were quite poor. We had hoped for better results than these, but as we note in the footnote to Table 6.2, the inclusion of a lagged dependent variable improves matters tremendously.

The value of U for property was to be expected from the good fits achieved in the equations run and likewise for house purchase loans. What is surprising is the relatively poor showing of debentures. With fits of 80 per cent we might have expected a slightly better performance in terms of predictive power. For short-term assets the values of U are suggestive of being no better than a zero change extrapolation.

In Table 6.3 we give the results for these equations re-estimated for the whole data period 1963-76. The decrease in fit on the debentures equation is a symptom perhaps of the relatively high value of U obtained in the prediction. The increase in the fit of gilts to 80 per cent is a notable feature, but short-term assets also record an increase on the fit. In the case of the latter, however, the Durbin-Watson statistic does give some cause for concern. Certainly the increase in fit is the result of the lagged dependent variable term and this, of course, does not allow us to place any credence in the unadjusted Durbin-Watson (DW) statistic.

6.3 Towards an Overall Model

We recognise the need to combine these individual demand specifications with an overall portfolio model of strategic investment choice and allocation and this section is based on J.C. Dodds (50). The estimation used is OLS and the models we appraised in Chapter 4 utilised this. If the portfolio of life assets is to be seen as something overall, as we have suggested from Chapter 3, then we must produce a behavioural model. Whilst it is easy to state this (indeed we are stating the obvious), this final step of combining our asset demand equation is a particularly difficult task. It is just not possible to piece together the various equations without some changes. To be specific, the investment process we have argued is partly sequential in nature, whereby some assets, particularly loans and mortgages and corporate bonds, are taken first *ceteris paribus*, with the remaining funds being allocated among the other competing outlets. It is in this second part of the choice or allocation process that the problems we have alluded to arise. For consistency of estimation it is usual for the same set of independent variables to feature in each equation. This can present particular econometric problems for the estimation in terms, for instance, of the number of coefficients which can result in multi-collinearity and the like. This point has been recognised by others including B. Bosworth and J. Duesenberry (15). Our feelings are that whilst this does present the problems mentioned and it may well undo the careful work done at the individual specification level, a cost-benefit approach is necessary. Model building of this type is never an easy task and we have to recognise that we will inevitably lose some of the alleged behavioural aspects. For instance, in one of our specifications of the government securities, we have short-term assets as an independent variable, yet in the formal overall model we intend to explain the net acquisitions of these assets. On balance then we would argue for the same set of independent variables, but we recognise the problem with this approach.

One other factor that we have to consider is whether we can have the same asset groupings as before, particularly with regard to loans and

Table 6.3: Summary Equations for Individual Demand Specifications 1963-76

Equation number	6.3 (1)	6.3 (2)	6.3 (3)	6.3 (4)	6.3 (5)	6.3 (6)	6.3 (7)	6.3 (8)	6.3 (9)	6.3 (10)	6.3 (11)	6.3 (12)	6.3 (13)	6.3 (14)
Dependent variable	NA^C	NA^C	NA^C	NA^O	NA^G	NA^{GL}	NA^{GL}	NA^{LM}	NA^{OL}	NA^H	NA^P	NA^P	NA^{STA}	NA^{STA}
Variables														
Constant	22.5* (5.6)	16.9* (6.3)	8.24 (7.5)	18.7 (9.9)	14.7 (14.7)	15.4 (10.6)	8.9 (8.3)	10.5 (5.4)	8.6* (2.6)	45.4* (8.0)	−17.1* (7.4)	−3.0 (5.0)	−88.6* (37.6)	−68.2 (39.2)
I^C_t	0.3* (0.04)	0.33* (0.04)	0.29* (0.05)											
I^O_t		−0.008 (0.02)	−0.005 (0.02)	0.16* (0.05)										
I^G_t	0.01 (0.003)				0.10* (0.01)									
I^{GL}_t						0.34* (0.02)	0.24* (0.02)							
$(R^D - R^{O1})_{t-1}$				4.2 (2.5)										
$(R^D - R^L)_{t-1}$	0.6 (5.1)	6.2 (5.7)	7.4 (5.5)				0.27* (0.03)							
$(R^L - R^{O1})_{t-1}$					3.8 (3.4)	−4.8 (12.5)								
$(R^L - R^S)_{t-1}$													29.7* (12.2)	
$BSLiq_{t-1}$								−5.0* (1.4)		−2.72* (0.5)				0.5 (6.8)

TNA								−0.02* (0.01)	−0.03* (0.009)					
TNA^{AA1}				−0.02 (0.06)										
STA					0.29* (0.05)	0.2* (0.03)								
R^{STA}_{t-1}											3.4* (1.4)		12.4* (5.1)	12.6 (6.8)
HPI										0.03* (0.008)				
HPI$_{t-1}$											0.13* (0.04)	0.16* (0.04)		
$(R_P^L - R_P^O)_{t-1}$											−0.01 (0.05)	0.006 (0.05)		
ΣI_t													−2.1 (0.06)	
D(2)	−16.5* (5.0)	−22.8* (5.6)	−18.3* (5.8)				−15.3 (11.3)							
Lag of dependent variable			0.23* (0.11)	0.19 (0.14)				0.8* (0.08)	0.6* (0.1)	0.62* (0.07)	0.28* (0.14)	0.4* (0.1)	0.7* (0.1)	0.9* (0.1)
$\bar{R}^2$	0.85	0.74	0.76	0.32	0.80	0.93	0.92	0.70	0.62	0.79	0.87	0.86	0.82	0.79
DW	1.6	1.3	1.5	0.9	2.4	1.9	1.7	2.0	1.9	2.0	2.1	2.0	2.9	2.8
Det. C	0.1	0.4	0.2	0.2	0.4	0.3	0.3	0.9	0.9	0.7	0.1	0.3	0.9	0.9

mortgages and government securities. Whilst the arguments for disaggregation are very compelling, we would certainly not wish to aggregate to the extent of say the Munro model discussed in Chapter 4.

In Table 6.4[2] we present our results for version 1 (static) of our overall model. We posit that loans and mortgages have the first choice over the available funds and corporate bonds the second. We can note that we have not included an income constraint here. Our argument for this is that life offices have, over our data period consistently had a positive inflow of funds sufficient to meet any anticipated needs for these assets. The constraints on net acquisitions will come from either the supply side, that is the availability of these assets and/or from the existing stock position *vis-à-vis* the desired or target portfolio. This portfolio will depend, as was argued earlier, on a series of factors including the liability mix and the characteristics of the assets themselves. We attempt to capture this, as before, by the inclusion of a lagged dependent variable in version 2.

The real difficulty in the analysis comes with the second set of assets that compete among themselves for the available funds. These funds are not of course the total net acquisitions but are adjusted for the prior net acquisitions of loans and mortgages and corporate bonds. As these assets include fixed interest (gilts) and variable return (ordinary shares and property) then we need to capture some of the strategic choice here and the reverse yield gap worked well in Chapter 5. In some previous formulations, we used the price indices version, particularly in the property equations, whereas in others we used the straight yields. For consistency, given the use of yields in the corporate bond equation we ought to use yields and this we do. However, we did estimate an alternative version which had prices and we are pleased to report that the results were virtually identical. For property the house price index is included, and we also include a short-rate (R^{STA}) lagged one period as the own yield on the short-term assets. As there are also supply constraints in at least two markets, gilts and ordinary shares, then the issues of these in t are also included. Version 1 is a 'flow' model and version 2 (Table 6.5) allows for the partial stock adjustment mechanism to be at work. Both versions have a sequential allocation process.

In version 1 we can see that for the debentures we use an equation which not only includes the issues and the shift dummy, but the two yield gaps. The reasoning for this is that whilst we are arguing that the allocation to debentures is prior to that of the other assets, it is still a choice asset to be considered on the basis of yields. For loans and mortgages we have building society liquidity as the sole argument.

The reason for this is that the lagged dependent variable will be included in version 2 and the income constraint of *TNA* we are positing is not really applicable to first choice assets, Nevertheless the result is quite encouraging. In the second set of competitive assets, the results are rather disappointing and statistically insignificant coefficients abound, though this was to be expected. The Durbin-Watson statistics are good apart from in the property equation and the multi-collinearity as measured by Det. *C* is relatively low. If we take the four assets sequentially, then for ordinary shares, the relationship is little different from that found in Table 6.1. The inclusion of the issues of government securities produces the expected negative sign, but the coefficient is not significant at the 5 per cent level. The inclusion of a short-rate lagged one period produces the correct *a priori* sign, but is insignificant at the 5 per cent level but the reverse yield gap is significant (at the 5 per cent level) and of the sign rationalised in Chapter 5. One additionally good factor is the statistical significance of the adjusted income series. The fit is still obstinately low at 0.65. For property, the inclusion of the issues of the other two assets produces a negative sign on equity (I_t^O) and a positive sign on gilts (I_t^G). The coefficient on I_t^O is significant, as are the own yield term (HPI) and short-term asset rate (R^{STA}). The sign is positive which is in line with the previous property equations. This is suggestive of a situation that when short-term rates are rising and there is perhaps less interest in marketable securities, net acquisitions of property will increase. The adjusted income series is both insigificant and has a perverse sign. For gilts the fit slumps again from that which we have been able to obtain previously on individual specifications. The only coefficient significant of the independent variables is the supply constraint. Turning to the short-term assets equation, the coefficients on the issues of both ordinary shares and gilts are negative (as we would expect) but only the latter is significant. The own yield is positively signed, but not significant, however, the reverse yield gap is and negatively signed. The adjusted income series is correctly signed and significant. The overall fit is relatively low though higher than that obtained in previous individual demand formulations.

Turning to version 2, which for want of a better word, we refer to as 'dynamic', we can see that this does improve the relationship specified for loans and mortgages; but that in the second set of assets there are very few differences to be noted. Two of the lags are significant — ordinary shares and property — and this was to be expected from previous demand specifications. The Durbin-Watson statistics do, apart

Table 6.4: Life Insurance Companies — 1963-74 — Version 1 (Static)

Equation number	6.4 (1)	6.4 (2)	6.4 (3)	6.4 (4)	6.4 (5)	6.4 (6)
Variables						
Dependent variable	NA^C	NA^{LM}	NA^O	NA^P	NA^G	NA^{STA}
Constant	24.6* (5.9)	181.1* (24.2)	38.3* (15.3)	−21.0* (6.0)	46.0* (19.9)	−77.3* (28.1)
I^C_t	0.24* (0.04)					
I^O_t			0.20* (0.08)	−0.05* (0.02)	0.04 (0.13)	−0.13 (0.15)
I^G_t			−0.01 (0.01)	0.002 (0.004)	0.07* (0.01)	−0.06* (0.02)
HPI_{t-1}			−0.14 (0.15)	0.22* (0.06)	−0.05 (0.19)	0.08 (0.27)
R^{STA}_{t-1}			−6.3 (3.3)	3.7* (1.3)	−5.97 (4.0)	11.9 (6.3)
$(R^D - R^L)_{t-1}$	1.7 (1.4)					
$(R^D - R^{01})_{t-1}$	−3.2 (5.3)					
$(R^L - R^{01})_{t-1}$			8.5* (3.1)	2.3 (1.2)	7.3 (4.0)	−20.3* (5.7)
TNA^{AA1}			0.27* (0.11)	−0.01 (0.03)	0.05 (0.1)	0.78* (0.2)
$D(2)$		−25.1* (6.8)				
$BSLiq_{t-1}$		−9.0* (1.5)				
$\bar{R}^2$	0.77	0.44	0.65	0.88	0.51	0.56
DW	1.9	1.2	1.9	1.5	2.0	1.9
Det. C	0.09	1.0	0.41	0.01	0.01	0.01

Table 6.5: Life Insurance Companies — 1963-74 — Version 2 (Dynamic)

Equation number	6.5 (1)	6.5 (2)	6.5 (3)	6.5 (4)	6.5 (5)	6.5 (6)
Variables						
Dependent variable	NA^C	NA^{LM}	NA^O	NA^P	NA^G	NA^{STA}
Constant	24.2* (8.0)	84.9* (27.5)	30.0* (15.0)	−16.4* (6.6)	46.9* (20.3)	−7.9* (2.8)
I_t^C	0.25* (0.04)					
I_t^O			0.18* (0.08)	−0.04 (0.03)	0.05 (0.1)	−0.13 (0.14)
I_t^G			−0.01 (0.005)	0.003 (0.004)	0.07* (0.01)	−0.06* (0.02)
HPI_{t-1}			−0.1 (0.1)	0.19* (0.06)	−0.06 (0.19)	0.06* (0.03)
R^{STA}_{t-1}			−4.8 (3.3)	2.5* (1.3)	−6.1 (4.4)	10.3 (6.3)
$(R^D - R^L)_{t-1}$	−3.0 (5.4)					
$(R^D - R^{01})_{t-1}$	17.2* (1.4)					
$(R^L - R^{01})_{t-1}$			6.6* (3.2)	1.91 (1.16)	7.4 (4.1)	−20.5* (5.6)
TNA^{AA1}			0.21* (0.10)	−0.06 (0.04)	0.07 (0.1)	0.7* (0.2)
$BSLiq_{t-1}$		−4.3* (1.5)				
$D(2)$	−24.8* (7.2)					
Lag of dependent variable	0.02 (0.1)	0.6* (0.1)	0.23* (0.11)	0.28* (0.12)	−0.04 (0.1)	−0.22* (0.2)
$\bar{R}^2$	0.76	0.63	0.67	0.89	0.50	0.57
DW	1.9	2.1	2.2	2.2	2.0	1.6
Det. C	0.02	0.6	0.005	0.002	0.009	0.01

Table 6.6: Predictive Performance of Overall Models Explaining the Asset Demand Behaviour of Life Insurance Companies 1975 (1) — 1977 (4)[a]

Models	1975 (1) — 1976 (4)		1977 (1) — 1977 (4)	
	Static	Dynamic	Static	Dynamic
Variables predicted				
Debentures	0.6538	0.6384	0.9622	0.8714
Loans and mortgages	0.5368	0.3635	0.3078	0.8173
Ordinary shares	0.3676	0.3721	0.9555	0.9730
Property	0.1186	0.1039	0.1758	0.1977
Government securities	0.4271	0.4226	0.4343	0.4679
Short-term assets	0.5539	0.6073	0.6487	0.6950

a. All elements are values of U.

from short-term assets, appear to be biased by the inclusion of the lagged variable. Another feature is that the multi-collinearity starts to increase in this model.

We tested for the predictive power of both versions and these results are contained in Table 6.6. The findings here are of the same magnitude as those of Table 6.2, except that whilst in the case of short-term assets, U improves, for gilts it declines. For the sake of completeness, we also estimated both versions of our overall model for the full data period up to 1976 and we give these in Tables 6.7 and 6.8 and the predictions in Table 6.6. If we compare static with static there are three asset classes whose results do improve markedly, namely loans and mortgages, government securities and short-term assets. These all now feature very good statistical fits. The same thing is repeated in the dynamic and the fit on short-term assets now reaches 0.91 with all but two coefficients significant at the 5 per cent level and one of these two (R_{t-1}^{STA}) is significant at the 10 per cent level. So the extension of our data period does, on balance, improve the performance of our overall model and our individual demand specifications (Table 6.3), though we can note the increase in multi-collinearity, in both static and dynamic versions.

In building these overall models, we can see the proliferation of insignificant coefficients we have referred to earlier and that in some particular assets, particularly gilts, we cannot do as well as the individual demand specifications. Indeed on long bonds in Table 6.3, Equation

Table 6.7: Life Insurance Companies 1963-76 — Version 1 (Static)

Equation number	6.7 (1)	6.7 (2)	6.7 (3)	6.7 (4)	6.7 (5)	6.7 (6)
Variables						
Dependent variable	NA^C	NA^{LM}	NA^O	NA^P	NA^G	NA^{STA}
Constant	19.2* (7.6)	177.5* (16.6)	64.5* (12.9)	−23.4* (5.3)	−17.2 (27.2)	−189.0* (30.6)
I_t^C	0.32* (0.05)					
I_t^O			0.09* (0.04)	−0.005 (0.02)	0.16 (0.09)	0.48* (0.1)
I_t^G			−0.02* (0.006)	−0.001 (0.003)	0.1* (0.01)	−0.002 (0.02)
HPI_{t-1}			−0.06 (0.13)	0.29* (0.05)	0.03 (0.3)	−0.07 (0.3)
R_{t-1}^{STA}			−10.4* (3.2)	2.9* (1.3)	1.7 (6.4)	26.0* (7.5)
$(R^D-R^L)_{t-1}$	6.5 (5.6)					
$(R^D-R^{01})_{t-1}$	−0.94 (1.5)					
$(R^L-R^{01})_{t-1}$			13.3* (2.3)	2.3* (1.1)	−7.4 (5.8)	−38.4* (6.6)
TNA^{AA1}			0.11 (0.07)	−0.09* (0.03)	0.37* (0.16)	1.1* (0.18)
$D(2)$	−19.4* (8.4)					
$BSLiq_{t-1}$		−8.7* (1.0)				
$\bar{R}^2$	0.75	0.59	0.61	0.89	0.79	0.88
d	1.3	1.1	1.6	1.7	2.5	1.5
Det. C	0.1	1.0	0.002	0.002	0.002	0.002

Table 6.8: Life Insurance Companies 1973-76 — Version 2 (Dynamic)

Equation number	6.8 (1)	6.8 (2)	6.8 (3)	6.8 (4)	6.8 (5)	6.8 (6)
Variables						
Dependent variable	NA^C	NA^{LM}	NA^O	NA^P	NA^G	NA^{STA}
Constant	9.5 (8.8)	82.7* (20.7)	48.0* (14.5)	−17.2* (5.8)	−19.0 (27.3)	−138.2* (29.3)
I_t^C	0.29* (0.05)					
I_t^O			0.1* (0.04)	−0.0002 (0.02)	0.21* (0.1)	0.3* (0.1)
I_t^G			−0.02* (0.007)	−0.001 (0.003)	0.10* (0.01)	−0.03 (0.02)
HPI_{t-1}			−0.06 (0.12)	0.23* (0.06)	−0.04 (0.3)	−0.25 (0.27)
R_{t-1}^{STA}			−7.4* (3.3)	1.6 (1.3)	2.4 (6.6)	22.3* (6.5)
$(R^D - R^L)_{t-1}$	7.6 (5.5)					
$(R^D - R^{01})_{t-1}$	−0.5 (1.4)					
$(R^L - R^{01})_{t-1}$			9.9* (3.1)	2.3* (1.1)	7.7 (5.8)	−29.1* (6.1)
TNA^{AA1}			0.08 (0.07)	−0.09* (0.03)	0.46* (0.19)	0.9* (0.2)
$D(2)$	−16.6* (8.3)					
$BSLiq_{t-1}$		−4.2* (1.1)				
Lag of dependent variable	0.23* (0.11)	0.6* (0.1)	0.25* (0.11)	0.27* (0.12)	−0.16 (0.17)	0.38* (0.09)
$\bar{R}^2$	0.76	0.75	0.64	0.90	0.79	0.91
d	1.5	2.1	2.0	2.2	2.5	2.2
Det. C	0.2	0.5	0.0007	0.0004	0.0006	0.0007

6.3 (6) we cannot hope to improve much on a fit of 0.93, though we recognise that for the reduced data period the fit does fall. But our point is that in our modelling of the sector as a sector, a cost-benefit approach is necessary, and in going for more completeness we have to sacrifice some other behavioural aspects. Nevertheless, we would hope that the results presented in this chapter are in themselves quite encouraging. Certainly they would appear to be 'better' than those reported in Chapter 4 and we have attempted in this study to justify the inclusion of the various arguments in the equations. If predictive power is the test of the models, *a la* Friedman (62), then again our models would appear to have strong validity. Having said that, we are conscious that these are still far from perfect and that further work is necessary and it is to this aspect that we turn our attention in Chapter 7.

Notes

1. We follow our usual practice as regards the layout of the tables and the statistics. However, we could have made use of an additional statistic namely that of residual variance. K.M. Garver and M.S. Geisel (67) give an excellent review of the literature on this matter. The argument that can be put forward is that model builders should choose models with the lowest S^2 (residual variance) in preference to $\bar{R}^2$. There are two further points here. In the first instance H. Theil (159) has argued that on average $\bar{R}^2$ will in fact choose the correct model and also in the main in our own case the larger $\bar{R}^2$ did coincide with a lower S^2 between equations. In consequence, we do not quote this statistic.

2. We should really estimate an equation for the residual assets to close this model. However, we cannot specify any meaningful demand equation for this.

7 CONCLUSIONS

In this chapter we wish to offer an overview or perspective on our study as well as to indicate areas for further work. The focus of the study has been to take the life insurance industry as a sector rather than to adopt a company or cross-section approach. We set ourselves the task within this context of marshalling the facts on the portfolio composition of life offices, including their position in financial markets and examining the principles which appeared to underlie the investment process. We then set out to model their net acquisition utilising as much of the behavioural inputs as we could. In this last respect we are following many other researchers in the field of financial institutions, including ourselves, but we indicated the lack of work on the life insurance sector. This has been both a handicap and an advantage. It has been an advantage in that there has been virtually no work to survey and this has forced us back, as it were, to first principles and necessitated the building block approach which is what we have attempted to do in this present study. The handicaps have been that this has involved us in a lot of description and analysis before we felt we could start any econometric work. In consequence the study is perhaps longer than we might have expected *a priori* and in addition it is weighted differently. In other words a similar study of banks would have involved a far greater analysis of other empirical work by virtue of the abundance of the literature, particularly in the USA.

What this study has confirmed is the Joan Robinson assertion that there is 'no knock down answer'. Whilst we recognise that economics as a discipline is striving to propound testable hypotheses, we are faced at times with the charge that we are not in a position to say anything positive. But in empirical work a start has to be made somewhere and some of the undergrowth surrounding a problem has to be cleared before econometric testing can proceed. Indeed, we have made the charge earlier in this study that in the past, it would appear that relatively sophisticated techniques have been applied to the investment and portfolio management of financial institutions without due regard for the nature of the institution concerned. There has often been no feel for the data. The latter have been seen as a mere (but essential) input to which can be applied the notable advances made in recent years in the econometric analysis of models. We have therefore illustrated the great difficulties that face model builders, particularly in the life insurance sector. By exposing them we cannot claim that we have necessarily handled these sufficiently well or even taken them fully into account, but we hope in this chapter to illustrate where further developments might lead.

Our main problems have come in using the theoretical frameworks available to us to model life office investment. Arguing that investment managers will be concerned broadly to match assets to their liability structure, yet stand willing to trade, presents us with the difficulty of providing the data on this liability structure and the changes in it. We did try some specifications, but they were not particularly successful, and in consequence we have found it virtually impossible to test for a matching or immunisation investment strategy. Instead we have to argue that the liability structure will be contained in the desired portfolio, which itself is not observable and we capture adjustments via a one-period lag of the dependent variable. This is a very mechanical approach to an important prop to the investment allocation process of life offices. Yet one which at present we have been forced to take. In fact the long and elaborate building block approach used in previous chapters produces a mongrel set of models in Chapter 6. This is disappointing and if these models were to be taken in isolation, they may appear to lack any behavioural validity, although their predictive power is quite encouraging. If these overall models are evaluated in conjunction with the individual specifications of Chapter 5 and the analysis of previous chapters, then the reader may concur with the final approach we have adopted. However, this linking between individual asset demand functions and the final overall models is one which does require further analysis. The problems would be compounded even more if we intended to fit the life insurance industry as a sector into a large-scale financial model. Further aggregation and simplification would be necessary which could destroy the descriptive and explanative nature of the models, though they need not necessarily destroy all their predictive power.

Whilst the models we have adopted focus on strategic choices among asset classes, we have *en passant* as it were covered choice and switching within asset classes, though this again is an area which would repay a more detailed coverage. This would be only possible by virtue of data constraints on a micro basis with a few life offices. In part, a start was made on this by M.H. El-Habishi (55), using data from one company, though the intention of the study, as we have argued elsewhere, was to apply mathematical programming techniques to the selection decision.

Micro studies are certainly an area where further work will and needs to be done. In this we do lag behind the USA in that the early work of L. Wehrle (167) and interview and questionnaire studies by B.G. Malkiel (100) and E.J. Kane and B.G. Malkiel (89) gave valuable insights into individual company attitudes to various problems. Our own findings from discussions with investment managers in the UK and the work of G. Clayton and W.T. Osborn (33) and R.L. Carter and J.E.V. Johnson (27), all point to great differences in attitudes and portfolio composition among life offices.

The pioneering work of D.D. Hester and J.L. Pierce (81), whilst on commercial banks in the USA, still gives as a methodological base and a valuable guide to micro studies and to aggregating these to obtain a comparison with overall industry performance. Certainly, if the linkage between micro and macro models could be developed, then we could foresee having a detailed and comprehensive picture of the investment process in the life insurance sector. Detailed data are available on a company basis and provided the sample was carefully constructed, this could be a useful extension of research, though data difficulties might still remain, particularly on the specification of yields. In fact, data problems are usually the hallmark of model builders in economics, in that the techniques are often better than the data series used in the estimation. We have pinpointed several instances where we have found the shortage particularly acute. Some of these could be removed within the structure of the existing data series, particularly the provision of quarterly data on policies written; further disaggregation of the land, property and ground rent asset class and other loans and mortgage class. Others would be more difficult to remove, particularly the provision of yields on property and data on expectations of future policy income and on the expectations of future movements of interest rates. Simply to rely on various mechanistic schemes, naive or sophisticated, is only a proxy for expectation formation. We have, in the main, relied on 'static expectations' since there is some evidence to support this line of argument; though equally so we recognise that this is an assumption that can be severely questioned and censured. Our test on extrapolative and regressive schemes did not produce any meaningfully different results probably by virtue of the importance of near term yields. More effort needs to be concentrated in this area particularly with regard to holding period yields. The approach of J.R. Hemsted (78) (79) is a particularly useful development and certainly an area that we intend to follow up in future work.

The research into the life insurance sector at an industry level does indicate that a wealth of work still remains to be done. We recognise that further refinement and improvements of our models would be possible and indeed the whole concept of a sequential investment process could still be questioned. If we accept the format of the approach taken, refinements could be made in the present model by estimating an equation for life insurance policy reserves and then re-estimating the model using two stage least squares and instrumental variables. Having gone so far as to estimate a simultaneous model of this type, it would be a logical step to develop linkages with the real sector of the economy, though we recognise the difficulties of this, given our own work on financial sector models. In consequence then, this present study has hopefully cleared some of the undergrowth surrounding the portfolio decisions of life offices and follow-up studies should find the guidelines established useful to build on and develop further.

APPENDIX

Table A1 (a): Life Insurance Companies' Holdings of Assets — Book Values 1961-76 (end year)[c]

Assets £m / Years	Total	UK short-term assets (net)	British govt. securities	Local authority securities	Overseas govt. securities	Company securities: Debentures	Pref. shares	Ordinary shares	Unit trust units	UK — loans and mortgages: Loans and mortgages	House purch. loans	Loans on companies policies	Other	Overseas	Land property and ground rent	Agents balances etc.	Other assets
Life funds																	
1961	6254	46	1594	308	82	817	331	1302		1035	634		388	13	619	89	31
1962	6785	51	1742	320	77	911	339	1399		1149	685		450	14	670	106	24
1963	7425	55	1882	347	76	1057	357	1538		1243	719		508	16	729	115	26
1964	8143	69	2001	350	77	1240	364	1731		1372	768		587	17	795	116	28
1965	8826	62	2086	378	73	1444	375	1821		1542	848		677	17	889	126	30
1966	9514	54	2132	372	70	1667	360	1948		1715	876		820	19	1007	149	40
1967	10626	91	2584	384	100	1908	299	2076		1836	909		905	22	1129	183	37
1968	11831	89	2782	405	101	2113	259	2580		2031	1021		986	24	1264	202	5
1969	12741	121	2952	391	88	2216	232	2837	35	2212	1080		1102	30	1452	220	22
1970	13781	233	3069	378	86	2305	206	3202	65	2332	1117		1186	29	1692	245	–
1971	15011	148	3542	364	88	2439	201	3552	105	2418	1132	(194)	1248	39	1932	263	–
1972	16574	263	3791	353	93	2555	185	4373	118	2432	1110	(188)	1283	39	2120	304	–
1973	18125	389	4156	358	96	2594	181	4597	414	2684	1218	(194)	1425	41	2636	315	
1973	19732	679	4308	379	98	2657	184	4856	446	2730	1229	(204)	1456	45	3082	336	9
1974	20718	1201	4465	518	91	2585	186	4258	454	2984	1381	(293)	1556	47	3558	405	21
1975	23842	950	5606	559	104	2617	166	5062	514	3016	1439	(264)	1558	50	4350	455	4
1976	25131	930	7206	534	129	2476	179	5160	515	2920	1447	(263)	1510	54	4462	472	155[b]
1976[a]	24487	930	4917	425	107	1753	115	6925	515	2920	NA	NA	NA	NA	5254	472	155

a. Market values, except for short-term assets and loans and mortgages.
b. Includes overseas property. This was previously included in land property and ground rents.
c. Other notes as for Table 2.8.

Source: As for Table 2.8.

Table A1 (b): Holdings by Life Insurance Companies of British
Government Securities[a] — by Maturity. Annual 1961-76 (end year)

	0—5	5—10	10—15	Over 15	Undated
1961	8	141	243	857	345
1962	10	73	199	1088	372
1963	38	94	188	1148	414
1964	37	73	172	1279	440
1965	37	162	183	1253	471
1966	28	81	200	1327	496
1967	92	92	189	1675	536
1968	70	75	187	1883	567
1969	50	78	222	2044	558
1970	44	141	184	2115	585
1971	57	168	129	2532	659
1972	89	167	148	2787	600
1973	83	296	576	2596	605
1973	107	326	599	2668	609
1974	147	341	573	2960	444
1975	395	309	538	3819	545
1976[b]	426	257	729	5372	421

a. Nominal values, £ million.
b. Given the revisions for 1976 for all government bonds for market values
given in Table A1 (a), then the data on a comparable basis by maturity would be
considerably less than that in this table; particularly the long (over 15) and
undated securities.
Source: Trade and Industry, HMSO.

Table A2 (a): Net Acquisitions — Cash Values Life Insurance Companies 1963-76[a]

Years	Total Assets £m	UK short-term assets (net)	British govt. securities	Local authority securities	Overseas govt. securities	Company securities: Debentures	Pref. shares	Ordinary shares	Unit trust units	Loans and mortgages	UK – loans and mortgages: House purch. loans	Loans on companies policies	Other	Overseas	Land property and ground rent	Agents balances etc.	Other assets
1963	586.0	1.0	110.0	25.0	2.0	145.0	22.0	119.0		92.0	32		59	1	60.0	9.0	-1.0
1964	631.0	16.0	92.0	–	-2.0	184.0	13.0	142.0		129.0	49		78	2	57.0	1.0	–
1965	633.4	-6.2	56.2	23.6	-3.9	207.9	1.7	71.5		179.1	87		91	1	92.9	10.0	0.6
1966	610.5	-14.5	28.4	-2.2	-4.2	233.5	-16.4	85.2		161.1	63		96	2	116.7	23.6	-0.7
1967	682.0	25.9	218.6	2.7	3.3	190.7	-43.9	61.2		92.0	33		57	2	103.5	28.2	-0.2
1968	790.9	-7.3	127.2	15.1	-1.8	213.9	-34.5	188.5		144.9	69		74	1	125.6	18.2	1.0
1969	751.0	34.7	119.7	-19.7	-11.4	117.5	-15.0	131.2		191.5	80		108	3.5	183.0	18.0	1.5
1970	816.5	90.8	84.2	-13.4	0.6	89.1	-18.5	232.4	9.0	113.9	34		78	2	202.6	25.8	-0.1
1971	970.9	-85.1	416.6	-12.9	-0.3	103.9	-6.3	295.3	10.3	43.3	11.3	0.2	30.1	1.7	189.0	17.3	-0.1
1972	1269.9	115.4	255.2	-9.1	3.8	149.4	-10.8	535.1	30.0	34.4	-20.8	-0.1	45.6	9.7	124.8	41.4	0.1
1973	1322.2	125.7	295.8	12.6	1.0	29.7	1.3	276.5	30.3	252.3	108.9	7.0	131.7	4.7	285.4	11.4	–
1974	1323.2	547.6	79.4	25.8	8.2	15.9	2.3	12.9	24.9	163.0	105.1	16.0	37.4	4.5	391.7	46.2	5.2
1975	1472.4	521.6	116.0	36.1	8.3	17.4	2.5	12.2	66.2	174.4	106.9	19.8	43.0	4.7	443.6	68.7	5.5
1976	1768.5	-250.3	1149.4	23.6	14.4	32.1	-2.5	213.7	75.1	60.0	57.7	4.5	-7.7	5.4	371.4	50.6	1.5
1977	2101.0	13.0	1511.7	42.8	2.4	-87.3	8.4	200.9	78.6	-39.5	8.3	-0.6	-51.5	4.3	386.5	50.6	-0.8

a. Notes as for Table 2.11, p. 55.

Source: Trade and Industry and Business Monitor M5, HMSO.

Table A2 (b): Net Investment of Life Insurance Companies in British
Government Securities — by Maturity, Cash Values (£ million) 1963-76

	Up to 5 years	Over 5 and up to 10 years	Over 10 and up to 15 years	Over 15 years	Undated
1963	22.0	−23.0	22.0	66.0	23.0
1964	−7.0	−14.0	−47.0	147.0	12.0
1965	−15.0	−12.0	37.0	35.0	12.0
1966	−12.1	−63.4	−62.4	157.1	9.7
1967[a]	−53.8	−2.3	16.0	257.6	0.9
1968	−34.7	−13.8	5.5	167.3	3.0
1969	−37.7	−21.2	21.3	152.3	4.9
1970	−15.9	11.7	27.2	45.8	15.4
1971	−9.0	−46.9	15.1	429.7	27.7
1972	32.2	−26.6	−5.9	282.4	−26.8
1973	−29.7	114.8	27.3	179.5	4.0
1974	9.7	14.1	−71.8	151.6	−24.0
1974[b]	8.6	53.2	−75.5	154.2	−24.4
1975	138.3	93.1	−51.1	946.3	22.8
1976	−34.2	40.9	147.6	1392.0	−34.6

a. From 1967 includes Commonwealth Life Funds.
b. Including an estimate for non-members of the British Insurance Association.

Table A3: Percentages of Total Assets of Ten Life Offices Invested in Different Classes of Securities: 1871 to 1952

End year	1871	1875	1880	1885	1890	1895	1898	1900	1905	1910	1915	1920	1925	1930	1935	1951	1952
British government securities	6.7	5.5	2.7	2.1	2.2	1.0	0.8	0.5	0.7	0.3	0.6	35.2	39.5	19.9	21.8	25.8	25.4
Commonwealth other than UK government securities											2.4	2.7	6.4	6.8	6.0	1.8	1.7
Commonwealth other than UK provincial securities	2.7	2.1	3.3	4.5	6.6	7.5	7.5	7.1	5.4	4.0	1.1	0.5	0.5	0.5	0.6	–	–
Commonwealth other than UK municipal securities[a]											4.9	2.3	1.8	2.0	1.8	0.3	0.3
Foreign municipal securities	–	–	–	0.2	0.4	2.0	4.4	4.8	4.9	5.5	2.4	0.5	0.5	0.8	0.3	–	–
Foreign government and provincial securities	0.1	0.9	0.3	0.1	0.1	0.3	0.8	1.6	1.5	2.1	2.6	1.9	3.3	5.1	3.1	0.6	1.2
Debenture and debenture stocks	7.5	7.9	4.2	5.7	5.0	11.2	16.2	18.1	22.9	28.8	29.7	11.7	9.6	14.3	15.7	12.4	12.4
Preference and guaranteed stocks and shares	1.6	3.4	2.5	3.2	3.4	3.4	5.9	6.9	7.2	7.8	5.1	3.3	3.1	9.1	8.5	11.2	10.5
Ordinary stocks and shares	9.1	11.4	11.5	9.9	9.1	9.8	7.8	7.2	5.8	4.4	2.0	1.7	1.1	5.0	7.5	20.1	20.6
Loans on rates, municipal and county securities and public boards – UK	2.1	3.1	3.0	3.9	3.8	3.1	2.9	5.8	3.6	3.2	2.7	2.3	2.9	3.4	5.3	3.4	3.0
Life interests and reversions and loans thereon	0.5	0.4	0.3	0.2	0.5	0.2	0.1	3.2	0.5	0.3	0.3	0.8	0.3	4.0	0.1	2.7	2.5
Loans on stocks and shares	7.9	7.0	6.9	6.9	6.5	6.5	6.3	6.7	7.9	9.2	9.8	8.5	8.1	11.4	7.6	1.7	1.9
Loans on policies within their surrender values	0.2	0.2	0.2	0.7	0.7	0.1	0.1	0.1	0.1	0.1	0.2	0.1	0.1	0.1	0.1	–	–
Loans on personal security	52.3	48.0	55.7	53.5	42.6	35.3	30.3	27.1	25.1	22.0	16.8	13.9	10.7	10.8	10.0	11.2	11.2
Mortgages on property within the UK	0.1	0.1	0.1	0.2	0.1	10.9	8.6	7.7	5.6	3.6	4.4	1.4	0.4	0.5	0.5	–	–
Mortgages on property out of UK	2.6	2.3	2.6	2.1	1.4	1.2	1.4	1.9	2.9	2.7	2.8	2.1	1.6	1.3	1.6	1.4	1.5
Rent charges, freehold and leasehold ground rents etc.	2.2	3.3	3.1	3.0	2.7	2.6	2.6	2.8	2.6	3.2	2.8	2.8	2.7	2.3	4.0	4.4	4.7
House property	1.7	1.6	1.0	1.5	4.8	2.5	1.7	1.4	1.0	0.6	1.0	0.9	0.5	0.1	0.5	0.9	1.1
Cash deposits and bank balances	2.7	2.8	2.6	2.3	2.4	2.4	2.6	2.3	2.3	2.2	2.2	1.9	1.9	2.0	1.8	2.0	1.9
Miscellaneous[b]																	

a. Prior to 1951 the Commonwealth government, provincial and municipal securities were classed as 'Indian and Colonial' and the debenture preference and ordinary stocks were classed as railway and other debentures and other debenture stocks and debenture stocks — home and foreign, railway and other preference and guaranteed stocks, railway and other guaranteed stocks, railway and other preferred ordinary and ordinary stocks and shares.

b. The row headed 'Miscellaneous' includes 'agent's balances', 'outstanding premiums', etc., and a few investment items (negligible in amount) where the heading in the Table under which they would be correctly included is not clear from the balance sheet descriptions.

Sources: A.C. Murray (111), p. 263 for the period 1871-1935 and C.M. Gulland (71) p. 412 for 1951 and 1952.

Table A4 (a): Life Insurance Companies' Net Investment in Assets as a Percentage of Total Net Acquisitions Quarterly 1963 (1) to 1976 (4)

Assets Period		BGS	LA	O	Company securities UT	P	D	LM	LPGR	OI	C
1963	1	25.5	2.8	13.6	—	2.2	23.4	11.6	11.4	−0.4	9.9
	2	26.7	0.9	18.0	—	4.8	21.6	19.1	10.4	—	−1.7
	3	23.3	8.8	24.9	—	4.5	22.6	16.9	10.9	0.5	−12.1
	4	3.2	4.6	24.8	—	3.4	32.4	16.3	9.1	1.0	5.2
1964	1	3.5	0.7	25.1	—	1.2	36.0	19.9	7.5	1.0	5.1
	2	18.2	1.8	24.0	—	3.3	23.6	15.4	7.0	−0.8	7.3
	3	17.6	—	21.5	—	2.7	26.8	16.6	7.3	−0.8	8.3
	4	19.5	−2.8	19.1	—	0.7	30.5	31.5	15.2	−0.8	−12.9
1965	1	13.2	8.5	14.9	—	0.7	32.7	25.0	13.3	−0.8	−7.4
	2	6.8	2.0	7.9	—	−3.2	22.9	34.9	15.9	−0.1	12.8
	3	0.9	0.9	12.7	—	2.7	42.1	32.4	18.3	−1.1	−8.7
	4	13.8	3.2	9.9	—	0.7	34.9	23.9	12.6	−0.1	1.2
1966	1	−10.9	5.2	17.0	—	0.1	43.8	27.1	13.6	−1.2	5.3
	2	4.8	1.1	16.9	—	−2.1	37.2	25.4	20.1	1.3	−4.7
	3	4.3	−3.1	13.9	—	−3.3	42.5	32.9	21.4	−3.8	−4.6
	4	22.3	−5.3	10.1	—	−6.2	35.5	25.2	25.2	—	−6.8
1967	1	36.3	1.3	4.3	—	−7.3	34.6	25.5	19.3	−0.2	−13.8
	2	21.9	4.9	4.9	—	−4.9	27.1	12.8	12.9	—	20.4
	3	35.4	−2.4	10.7	—	−7.0	22.6	10.4	14.7	−0.5	15.9
	4	40.3	−2.1	16.7	—	−7.7	32.7	8.9	16.8	2.4	−8.2
1968	1	23.3	0.9	25.7	—	−3.9	23.2	14.9	12.4	0.5	2.9
	2	19.8	5.3	35.2	—	−3.8	28.7	15.5	14.0	1.1	−15.8
	3	26.9	1.3	15.8	—	−4.1	29.5	20.8	18.0	−2.8	−5.5
	4	−5.2	0.7	21.0	—	−6.0	30.5	24.4	21.1	0.7	12.8
1969	1	−1.5	−1.5	20.8	—	—	40.5	31.1	26.3	1.6	−14.1
	2	19.5	−2.0	12.9	—	−0.2	17.7	27.9	20.0	1.8	5.8
	3	26.3	−3.9	17.5	—	−5.6	−7.4	23.6	27.7	2.6	24.4
	4	22.0	−3.8	21.7	—	−3.3	9.7	20.7	27.5	0.4	5.1
1970	1	24.4	−3.3	26.0	1.1	−3.3	12.3	19.6	34.9	1.5	−12.1
	2	−7.4	−1.0	46.6	1.2	−1.4	13.4	9.8	22.7	−0.6	16.5
	3	7.5	−2.9	23.2	1.2	−1.5	9.7	12.5	20.5	−0.6	30.2
	4	19.4	—	21.0	1.1	−3.2	9.8	16.2	25.3	0.9	9.5
1971	1	81.4	−1.1	19.6	0.8	−0.5	7.2	13.3	21.9	−0.7	−41.9
	2	26.7	−1.0	32.7	0.9	−0.5	10.9	4.6	16.9	−0.2	8.9
	3	48.4	−0.9	32.2	1.0	−0.5	19.2	0.9	17.7	−0.8	−17.2
	4	25.8	−2.3	38.2	1.6	−1.1	6.0	1.1	23.4	1.3	6.2
1972	1	40.4	−1.1	36.3	1.3	−1.4	15.9	−0.7	8.9	0.3	—
	2	15.6	−0.2	58.9	2.2	−0.8	12.2	−1.3	2.0	−0.7	12.1
	3	9.4	−1.5	55.2	3.3	−1.8	9.7	8.9	16.2	0.2	0.4
	4	19.4	−0.4	26.9	3.2	0.3	11.7	4.9	14.7	1.5	17.8
1973	1	16.9	0.2	22.0	2.4	1.2	2.1	15.6	18.2	—	21.4
	2	33.9	−1.2	7.8	2.4	−0.1	2.1	18.3	20.5	0.5	16.6
	3	16.3	2.5	16.7	2.1	0.8	−0.3	23.6	21.2	—	18.7
	4	23.1	2.4	37.4	2.3	2.3	5.0	19.8	27.3	0.8	−18.1
1974	1	0.2	7.0	6.5	1.6	1.2	0.9	16.2	22.3	0.9	43.3
	2	54.3	−0.1	12.1	5.8	−0.1	9.9	14.5	39.8	−1.2	−34.9
	3	−3.2	1.0	3.6	5.5	—	−0.2	14.3	34.6	1.9	42.4
	4	−16.8	−0.3	−17.1	4.3	−0.5	−3.8	5.9	33.1	1.6	93.6
1975	1	93.7	0.3	−6.5	4.2	−0.9	−2.7	6.2	25.7	2.6	−21.9
	2	38.8	4.9	24.3	3.7	0.3	2.9	5.2	20.6	0.8	0.02
	3	67.3	0.2	21.1	2.6	0.4	9.3	1.3	26.6	0.2	−30.5
	4	72.8	6.2	8.8	6.5	−0.5	−1.5	1.6	15.8	0.6	−10.3
1976	1	55.9	0.5	10.1	4.6	−0.6	1.1	1.2	13.8	0.5	12.8
	2	70.3	5.1	16.4	5.2	−1.5	−1.4	−1.9	24.3	—	−16.5
	3	49.2	2.0	11.4	3.0	3.6	−3.6	−3.4	18.7	−0.7	19.8
	4	117.3	0.1	0.2	2.1	−0.4	−13.4	−3.7	17.3	0.6	−20.8

Table A4 (b): Life Insurance Companies: British Government Securities — Maturities as a Percentage of Total Net Acquisitions (Cash Value) Quarterly 1963-76

Maturity		Shorts Lives up to 5 years	Mediums Lives from 5 up to 15 years	Longs Lives over 15 years	Undated	All securities
1963	1	7.9	−7.8	21.4	4.0	25.5
	2	−0.1	2.5	17.1	7.2	26.7
	3	8.6	5.7	7.9	1.1	23.3
	4	−1.0	−1.6	1.5	4.3	3.2
1964	1	3.9	−4.0	−1.1	4.6	3.4
	2	−5.3	−1.2	21.0	3.7	18.2
	3	−0.5	3.1	13.2	1.7	17.5
	4	−2.5	−41.2	66.1	−2.9	19.5
1965	1	−6.9	12.4	8.9	−1.2	13.2
	2	2.8	−2.1	8.9	−2.8	6.8
	3	−8.5	−0.2	1.7	7.9	0.9
	4	3.0	4.4	3.0	3.4	13.8
1966	1	−3.0	−22.1	10.5	3.6	−11.0
	2	−2.8	−9.1	13.5	3.2	4.8
	3	−4.5	−18.1	26.1	0.8	4.3
	4	1.8	−35.4	57.0	−1.1	22.3
1967	1	−0.9	−12.8	46.3	3.7	36.3
	2	17.2	3.9	9.8	−9.0	21.9
	3	−35.4	13.3	54.1	3.4	35.4
	4	−13.8	2.2	48.7	3.2	40.3
1968	1	−4.7	−1.1	25.7	3.4	23.3
	2	−10.2	3.5	25.1	1.4	19.8
	3	−2.6	−9.7	37.5	1.8	27.0
	4	−0.6	3.0	−2.0	−5.6	−5.2
1969	1	−8.3	0.8	−4.1	10.0	−1.6
	2	0.3	3.3	20.2	−4.4	19.4
	3	−7.8	−2.7	36.0	0.9	26.4
	4	−6.3	−2.6	33.9	−3.0	22.0
1970	1	−1.6	3.6	21.6	0.7	24.4
	2	0.5	14.0	−17.9	−3.9	−7.3
	3	−3.1	6.5	−2.9	7.0	7.5
	4	−3.8	−4.1	23.2	4.1	19.4
1971	1	−4.1	19.2	61.9	4.4	81.4
	2	6.0	−14.2	32.8	2.1	26.7
	3	−9.7	−11.7	66.5	3.3	48.4
	4	3.6	−3.2	23.2	2.1	25.7
1972	1	−0.6	−16.6	47.7	9.9	40.4
	2	7.6	0.3	7.9	−0.2	15.6
	3	0.6	7.9	8.6	−7.7	9.4
	4	2.7	−2.3	29.8	−10.5	19.4
1973	1	−7.1	6.2	20.0	−2.2	16.9
	2	11.1	21.2	3.3	−1.6	34.0
	3	−4.3	7.4	6.1	7.0	16.3
	4	−8.6	8.7	24.5	−1.5	23.1
1974	1	4.9	−2.4	−4.4	2.2	0.2
	2	4.7	26.0	23.8	−2.3	54.3
	3	0.1	−18.0	15.3	−0.6	−3.2
	4	−8.5	−16.7	16.3	−6.7	−16.8
1975	1	56.7	13.4	21.8	1.6	93.6
	2	3.0	−5.6	40.1	1.1	38.7
	3	−23.4	−14.2	103.5	1.5	67.2
	4	−1.0	15.0	55.3	1.0	72.8
1976	1	−9.1	26.3	39.7	−1.0	55.9
	2	−2.4	−3.2	74.4	1.5	70.3
	3	−4.1	7.2	64.1	−3.4	49.2
	4	10.8	18.7	90.5	−3.2	117.2

REFERENCES

1. Almon, S., 'The Distributed Lag between Capital Appropriations and Expenditures', *Econometrica* 33, no. 1, January|1965, pp. 179-81.
2. Ammeter, H., 'The Problem of Solvency in Life Assurance', *Journal of the Institute of Actuaries*, vol. 92, 1966, pp. 193-7.
3. Anderson, J.L. and Binns, J.D., 'The Actuarial Management of a Life Office', *Journal of the Institute of Actuaries*, vol. 83, 1957, pp. 112-52.
4. Ansoff, H.I., *Corporate Strategy* (McGraw Hill, 1965; Penguin, 1968).
5. Bailey, A.H., 'On the Principles on which the Funds of Life Assurance Societies should be Invested', *Journal of the Institute of Actuaries*, 1862.
6. Bank of England, *Quarterly Bulletin*, Official Transactions in the Gilt-edged Market, vol. 6, no. 2.
7. Barr, N., 'Real Rates of Return to Financial Assets since the War', *Three Banks Review*, vol. 107, September 1975, pp. 23-40.
8. Barrow, G.E., 'Actuaries and Long-term Insurance Business. Introductory Notes of a Sessional Meeting 26.1.1976', *Journal of Institute of Actuaries*, 1976, pp. 137-66.
9. Bayley, G.V. and Perks, W., 'A Consistent System of Investment and Bonus Distribution', *Journal of the Institute of Actuaries*, vol. 79, 1953, pp. 14-73.
10. Beard, R.E., 'Three R's of Insurance – Risk, Retention and Reinsurance', *Journal of the Institute of Actuaries Students Society*, vol. 15, 1960, pp. 399-421.
11. Benjamin, S., 'The Theory of Games and its Application to Rate of Interest', *Journal of the Institute of Actuaries*, vol. 85, 1959, pp. 373-437.
12. Bird, S., 'Inflation and the Return on Securities – A Comment', *Lloyds Bank Review*, April 1977, no. 124, pp. 44-5.
13. Bishop, G.A., *The Response of Life Insurance Investments to Changes in Monetary Policy, 1965-1970* (New York, Life Insurance Association of America, 1971).
14. Borch, K., 'Capital Markets and the Supervision of Insurance Companies', *Journal of Risk and Insurance*, pp. 397-414.
15. Bosworth, B. and Duesenberry, J.S., 'A Flow of Funds Model and its Implications in Issues in Federal Debt Management', *Federal Reserve Bank of Boston Conference Series*, no. 10, Boston, 1973.
16. Brainard, W.C., 'Financial Intermediaries and a Theory of Monetary Control', in *Financial Markets and Economic Activity*, Hester, D.D., and Tobin, J. (eds.) (New York, J. Wiley, 1967), pp. 94-141.
17. Brainard, W.C., and Tobin, J., 'Pitfalls in Financial Model Building', *AER*, PP. May 1963.
18. Bridge, J., and Dodds, J.C., *Planning and the Growth of the Firm* (London, Croom Helm, 1978).
19. Brimmer, A.F., *Life Insurance Companies in the Capital Market* (Michigan State University, 1962).
20. British Bond Ratings, *Exposure Draft, Investment Analyst*, December 1974, pp. 17-26.
21. British Bond Ratings, 'A Reply', *Investment Analyst*, 1976, pp. 5-16.
22. Britt, K.J., 'The Development of Industrial Assurance in Great Britain since

1928', in *Proceedings of the Centenary Assembly of the Institute of Actuaries*, vol. III.

23. Cagan, P., Chapter II in M. Friedman (ed.), *Studies in the Quantity Theory of Money* (Chicago, University of Chicago Press, 1956).

24. Carr, J.L., 'Yield Difficulties and Inflation, 1960-74', *Investment Analyst*, Sept. 1975, pp. 30-5.

25. Carter, R.L., *Economics and Insurance. An Introduction to the Economic Aspects of Insurance* (Stockport, P.H. Press Ltd, 1972).

26. Carter, R.L. (ed.), *Handbook of Insurance* (Khwer-Harrop Handbooks, London, 1973).

27. Carter, R.L., and Johnson, J.E.V., 'The Investment Policy of British Life Offices. Discussion Paper No. 42' in *Industrial Economics* (University of Nottingham, 1976).

28. Clarke, H.G., 'A Broad Analysis of the Problem of the Investment of Life Funds', *Journal of the Institute of Actuaries*, vol. 80, 1954, pp. 335-64.

29. Clayton, G., 'Role of British Life Assurance Companies in the Capital Market', *Economic Journal*, vol. 61, 1951.

30. Clayton, G., *British Insurance* (Elek, London, 1971).

31. Clayton, G., Dodds, J.C., Ghosh, D., and Ford, J.L., 'An Econometric Model of the U.K. Financial Sector: Some Preliminary Findings', in H.G. Johnson and A.R. Nobay (eds.), *Issues in Monetary Economics* (Oxford, Clarendon Press, 1974).

32. Clayton, G., Dodds, J.C., Driscoll, M.J., and Ford, J.L., 'The Portfolio and Debt Behaviour of British Building Societies', *SUERF*, Series A, 16A, 1973, Holland.

33. Clayton, G., and Osborn, W.T., *Insurance Company Investment. Principles and Policy* (Allen and Unwin, London, 1965).

34. Cocks, G., 'An Objective Approach to the Analysis of Portfolio Performance', *Investment Analyst*, December 1972, pp. 3-7.

35. Cocks, G., 'On the Measurement of the Rate of Return and Choice of a Standard of Comparison for Portfolio Performance Analysis', *Investment Analyst*, September 1974, pp. 7-13.

36. Commission on Money and Credit, *Life Insurance Companies as Financial Institutions* (New Jersey, Prentice-Hall, 1962).

37. Cottrell, H.C., 'Discussion' on the paper by H.G. Clarke (28), *Journal of the Institute of Actuaries*, vol. 80, 1954, pp. 376-77.

38. Craig, M., 'Local Authorities: Living on Borrowed Time and Money', *The Bankers Magazine*, November 1975.

39. Cummins, J.D., *An Econometric Model of the Life Insurance Sector of the US Economy* (Lexington, Mass., 1975).

40. Day, J.G., 'Developments in Investment Policy During the Last Decade', *Journal of the Institute of Actuaries*, vol. 85, 1958, pp. 123-64.

41. Defoe, D., *An Essay upon Projects*, 1697. See H.E. Raynes (131).

42. De Leeuw, F., 'A Model of Financial Behaviour', in Duesenberry, J., Fromm, G., Klein, L.R., and Kuch, E. (eds.), *Brookings Quarterly Econometric Model of the United States* (Chicago, Rand McNally, 1965), pp. 465-530.

43. De Morgan, A., *Essay on Probabilities*, 1838.

44. De Zoete and Bevan, *Equity and Fixed Interest Investment 1919-1973* (London, 1973).

45. Dickinson, G.M., 'Determinants of Insurance Company Asset Choice', *The Withdean Papers*, no. 2, 1971.

46. Dietz, P.O., 'Objectives of Measuring Investment Performance and their Implications for Developing a Performance Model', *Investment Analyst*,

May 1972.
47. Dodds, J.C., 'The Demand for Financial Assets by the British Life Funds – A Comment', *Oxford Bulletin of Economics and Statistics*, vol. 57, no. 2, May 1975, pp. 159-64.
48. Dodds, J.C., 'A Suggestion for the Rehabilitation of A.H. Bailey's Canons', *Investment Analyst*, December 1977.
49. Dodds, J.C., '*Say's Law of Financial Markets*: Institutional Investors and the New Issues of Marketable Securities 1963-77. A Note', *Investment Analyst*, December 1978.
50. Dodds, J.C., *Econometric Modelling of the Investment Behaviour of British Life Offices, 1963-77*, Department of Economics, Working Paper 1979-06, McMaster University.
51. Dodds, J.C., and Ford, J.L., *Expectations Uncertainty and the Term Structure of Interest Rates* (London, Martin Robertson; New York, Barnes and Noble, 1974).
52. Duesenberry, J., *Business Cycles and Economic Growth* (New York, McGraw-Hill, 1958).
53. Dyson, E.J.W., and Elphinstone, D.W., 'The Expenses of British Life Offices', *Journal of the Institute of Actuaries*, vol. 85, 1959, pp. 211-42.
54. *Economist, The*, Annual Survey of Insurance.
55. El-Habishi, M.H.H., 'The Use of Mathematical Programming and Related Techniques by Life Assurance Companies in Selecting Investment Portfolio', PhD Thesis (University of Sheffield, 1977).
56. El-Mokadem, A.M., *Econometric Models of Personal Saving in the United Kingdom 1948-1966* (London, Butterworth, 1973).
57. Fisher, L., and Lorie, J.H., 'Some Studies of Variability of Returns on Investment in Common Stocks', *Journal of Business*, April 1970.
58. Fisher, H.F., and Young, J., *Actuarial Practice of Life Assurance* (Cambridge University Press, 1965).
59. Ford, A., 'Life Office Returns to the Department of Trade and Industry', *Journal of the Institute of Actuaries*, vol. 101, 1974, pp. 53-67.
60. Fox, E.A., 'Comparing Performance of Equity Pension Funds', *Financial Analysts Journal*, vol. 24, no. 5, Sept.–Oct. 1963, pp. 121-9.
61. Franklin, P.J.. and Woodhead, C., *The UK Life Assurance Industry. A Study in Applied Economics*, (Croom Helm, forthcoming).
62. Friedman, M., *Essays in Positive Economics* (Chicago, Chicago University Press, 1953).
63. Friedman, M., and Schwartz, A.J., *A Monetary History of the United States 1867-1960* (NBEA, New York, 1963).
64. Friend, E., Blume, M., and Crockett, J., *Mutual Finds and Institutional Investor. A New Perspective* (New York, McGraw-Hill, 1970).
65. Freund, R.J., 'Introduction of Risk into a Programming Model', *Econometrica*, July 1956, pp. 387-98.
66. Frost, R., 'The Growth of Investment by Institutions 1938-53', *Oxford Economic Papers*, vol. 7, 1955.
67. Garver, K.M., and Geisel, M.S., 'Discriminating among Alternative Models: Bayesian and Non-Bayesian Methods', in *Frontiers in Econometrics*, P. Zarembka (ed.) (New York, Academic Press, 1974).
68. Ghosh, D., *The Economics of Building Societies* (Westmead, Farnborough, Saxon House, 1974).
69. Goodhart, C.A.E., 'The Gilt-edged Market', reprinted in *Readings in British Monetary Economics*, H.G. Johnson and others (eds.) (Oxford, 1972), pp. 439-69.
70. Grant, A.T., 'Switching of British Government Securities', *The Investment Analyst*, 1962, pp. 14-29.

71.   Gulland, C.M., Correspondence with the Editor, *Transactions of Faculty of Actuaries*, vol. 20, p. 412.
72.   Gurley, J.G., and Shaw, E.S., *Money in a Theory of Finance* (The Brookings Institution, Washington, 1960).
73.   Halley, E., An Estimate of the Degrees of the mortality of mankind, drawn from curious tables of the births and funerals, at the City of Breslau; with an attempt to ascertain the price of annuities on lives. See H.E. Raynes (131).
74.   Haynes, A.T., Abstract of discussion following Suttie, T.R., (185), pp. 222-3.
75.   Haynes, A.T., and Kirton, R.J., Abstract of Discussion following J.L. Anderson (3), pp. 165-7.
76.   Haynes, A.T., and Kirton, R.J., 'The Structure of a Life Office', *Transactions of the Faculty of Actuaries*, Edinburgh, Scotland, vol. 21, 1953, pp. 141-97.
77.   Headon, R.S., and Lee, J.F., 'Life Insurance Demand and Household Portfolio Behaviour', *Journal of Risk and Insurance*, vol. 41, 1974, pp. 685-98.
78.   Hemsted, J.R., 'The Expected Yield on Ordinary Shares', *Journal of the Institute of Actuaries Students' Society*, vol. 16, March 1962, pp. 401-26.
79.   Hemsted, J.R., 'One Year Returns and the Degree of Risk', *Journal of the Institute of Actuaries*, vol. 95, December 1969, pp. 19-77.
80.   Hendriks, F., 'Contributions to the Early History of Life Insurance', *Journal of the Institute of Actuaries*, vols. II and IV.
81.   Hester, D.D., amd Pierce, J.L., *Bank Management and Portfolio Behaviour*, Cowles Foundation Monograph 25 (New Haven and London, Yale University Press, 1975).
82.   Hickman, W.B., *Corporate Bond Quality and Investor Experience* (Princeton, National Bureau of Economic Research, Princeton University Press, 1958).
83.   Hicks, Sir J.R., *Value and Capital*, 2nd edn. (Oxford, Clarendon Press, 1946).
84.   Hodgman, D.R., *Commercial Bank Loan and Investment Policy* (Illinois, University of Illinois Press, 1963).
85.   Houston, D.B., and Simon, R.M., 'Economics of Scale in Financial Intermediaries: A Study of Life Insurance', *Econometrica* 38, no. 6, November 1970, pp. 856-64.
86.   Hughes, M., 'The Determinants of the Reverse Yield Gap', *The Investment Analyst*, no. 49, December 1977, pp. 9-14.
87.   Johnston, J., and Murphy, G.W., 'The Growth of Life Actuaries in UK since 1880', *Manchester Statistical Society Transactions*, November 1956, pp. 1-76.
88.   Jones, L.D., *Investment Policies of Life Insurance Companies* (Boston: Division of Research, Harvard Business School, 1968).
89.   Kane, E.J. and Malkiel, B.G., 'The Term Structure of Interest Rates: An Analysis of a Survey of Interest Rate Expectations', *Review of Economics and Statistics*, August 1967, pp. 343-55.
90.   Keran, M.W., 'Expectations, Money and the Stock Market', *St Louis Federal Reserve Bank Review*, January 1971.
91.   Keynes, J.M., *A Treatise of Money*, vol. 1 (London, Macmillan, 1930).
92.   Kirton, R.J., Abstract of Discussion on A.C. Murray (111).
93.   Knight, F.H., *Risk Uncertainty and Profit* (Boston, Houghton Mifflin, 1921).
94.   Koyck, L.M., *Distributed Lags and Investment Analysis* (Amsterdam, North Holland, 1954).

95.   Leijonhufvud, A., *On Keynesian Economics and the Economics of Keynes.*
       A Study in Monetary Theory (New York, Oxford University Press, 1968).
96.   Lever, E.H., Comments on the paper by H.E. Raynes (127).
97.   Lindley, G.M., 'Pension Fund Performances — the Wood and the Trees',
       Investment Analyst, May 1975, pp. 13-15.
98.   Lintner, J., 'Inflation and Common Stock Prices in a Cyclical Context',
       NBER 53rd Annual Report, September 1973.
99.   McCahan, D. (ed.), *Investment of Life Insurance Funds* (Heuber Founda-
       tion Lectures, University of Pennsylvania Press, 1953).
100.   Malkiel, B.G., *The Term Structure of Interest Rates Expectations and
       Behaviour Patterns* (Princeton, New Jersey, Princeton University Press,
       1966).
101.   Markowitz, H., *Portfolio Selection: Efficient Diversification of Invest-
       ments* (New York, J. Wiley, 1959).
102.   Marris, R.L., *The Economic Theory of Managerial Capitalism* (London,
       Macmillan, 1967) (with corrections).
103.   Marshall, J.B., 'British Government Securities', *Transactions of the Faculty
       of Actuaries*, vol. 22, 1953/4, pp. 19-35.
104.   Mason, S., 'Information for Investment Decisions. How Efficiently is It
       Used?', *Investment Analyst*, September 1971, pp. 3-16.
105.   Mason, S., 'Diversification and Turnover of Equity Portfolios Among UK
       Institutional Investors', *Investment Analyst*, December 1972, pp. 8-17.
106.   Meiselman, D., *The Term Structure of Interest Rates* (Englewood Cliffs:
       Prentice-Hall, 1962).
107.   Merrett, A.J., and Sykes, A., 'Return on UK Equities and Fixed Interest
       Securities 1919-66', *District Bank Review*, vol. 158, 1966, pp. 29-44.
108.   Modigliani, F., and Sutch, R.S., 'Innovations in Interest Rate Policy',
       American Economic Review, Papers and Proceedings, May 1966, pp.
       178-97.
109.   Moody, P.E., 'Life Funds and Equity Investment', *Journal of the Institute
       of Actuaries*, vol. 90, 1964, pp. 175-210.
110.   Munro, A., *Investment Policy of UK Life Offices. A Flow of Funds Model*,
       Discussion Paper No. 29 (University of Stirling, 1974).
111.   Murray, A.C., 'The Investment Policy of Life Assurance Offices', *Tran-
       sactions of the Faculty of Actuaries*, vol. 16, 1936-38, pp. 247-63.
112.   Nicholson, W.E., 'A Macroeconomic Model of Household Asset Choice',
       PhD dissertation (Massachusetts Institute of Technology, 1970).
113.   Norton, W.E., 'An Econometric Study of the United Kingdom Monetary
       Sector, 1955-1966', unpublished PhD thesis (University of Manchester,
       1967).
114.   O'Leary, J.J., *Forward Investment Commitments of Life Insurance Com-
       panies. The Quality and Economic Significance of Anticipation Data*
       (National Bureau of Economic Research, Princeton, Princeton University
       Press, 1960).
115.   Parkin, J.M., 'Discount House Portfolio and Debt Selection Behaviour',
       Review of Economic Studies, vol. 37, October 1970, pp. 469-97.
116.   Parkin, J.M., Gray, M.R., and Barrett, R.J., 'The Portfolio Behaviour of
       Commercial Banks', in *The Econometric Study of the UK: Proceedings
       of the 1969 Southampton Conference*, Hilton, K., and Heathfield, D.F.
       (eds.) (London, Macmillan, 1970).
117.   Patinkin, D., 'Financial Intermediaries and the Logical Structure of Mone-
       tary Theory', *American Economic Review*, 1961, pp. 95-116; and
       reprinted in his *Studies in Monetary Economics* (Harper and Row, 1972).
118.   Patrick, F.D., and Scobbie, A., 'Some Aspects of Withdrawals in Ordinary

Life Business', *Transactions of the Faculty of Actuaries*, vol. XXXI, 1968-9, p. 53.

119. Pegler, J.B.H., 'The Actuarial Principle of Investment', *Journal of the Institute of Actuaries*, vol. 74, 1949, pp. 139-211.

120. Pepper, G.T., 'The Selection and Maintenance of a Gilt-Edged Portfolio', *Journal of the Institute of Actuaries*, vol. 90, 1964, pp. 63-103.

121. Pesando, J.E., 'The Interest Sensitivity of the Flow of Funds through Life Insurance Companies: An Econometric Analysis', *Journal of Finance*, vol. 29, September 1974, pp. 1105-21.

122. Petty, W., as quoted in H.E. Raynes (131).

123. Pinches, G.E., and Treischmann, J.S., 'The Efficacy of Alternative Models for Solvency Surveillance in the Insurance Industry', *Journal of Risk and Insurance*, pp. 563-75.

124. Polke, L.C., and Titford, G.J., 'Some Considerations Affecting the Investment Overseas of Life Funds', *Journal of the Institute of Actuaries*, vol. 88, 1962, pp. 49-73.

125. Potter, D.C.H., 'The Effect upon Life Assurance Companies of a Change in the Rate of Interest', *Proceedings of the Eleventh International Congress of Actuaries*, 1937, pp. 315-27.

126. Radcliffe Committee, *Report of the Committee on the Working of the Monetary System*, Cmnd. 827 (HMSO, 1959).

127. Raynes, H.E., 'The Place of Ordinary Stocks and Shares (as distinct from Fixed Interest bearing Securities) in the Investment of Life Assurance Funds', *Journal of the Institute of Actuaries*, vol. 59, 1928, pp. 21-50.

128. Raynes, H.E., 'Equities and Fixed Interest Stocks during Twenty-five Years', *Journal of the Institute of Actuaries*, vol. 68, 1937, pp. 483-510.

129. Raynes, H.E., *Principles of British Insurance* (London, Pitman, 1953).

130. Raynes, H.E., *Insurance* (London, Oxford University Press, 1960).

131. Raynes, H.E., *A History of British Insurance* (London, Pitman, 1948). 2nd edn., 1964.

132. Read, E.K., 'Life Office Property Investments', *Journal of the Institute of Actuaries*, vol. 87, 1961, pp. 275-313.

133. Redington, F.M., 'Review of the Principles of Life Office Valuation', *Journal of the Institute of Actuaries*, vol. 78, 1952, pp. 286-340.

134. Revell, J.R.S., *Changes in the Structure of Life Assurance 1952-68*, Economic Research Paper, FIN.1 (University College of North Wales, Bangor, 1970).

135. Revell, J.R.S., *The British Financial System* (Macmillan, London, 1973).

136. Revell, J.R.S., *Solvency and Regulation of Banks*, Bangor, Occasional Papers in Economics, Number 5 (University of Wales Press, 1975).

137. Richardson, I.G., 'Inflation and the Return on Securities', *Lloyds Bank Review*, no. 121, July 1976, pp. 19-21.

138. Richardson, I.G., 'A Reply', *Lloyds Bank Review*, no. 124, April 1977, p. 45.

139. Robertson, D.H., and Dennison, S.R., *The Control of Industry*, 1960.

140. Robertson, D.J., and Sturrock, I.L.B., 'Active Investment Policy Related to the Holding of Matched Assets', *Transactions of the Faculty of Actuaries*, vol. 22, 1953-4, pp. 36-67.

141. Robinson, J., 'The Rate of Interest', *Econometrica*, 17, April 1951, pp. 92-111.

142. Roy, A.D., 'Safety First and the Holding of Assets', *Econometrica*, 1952, pp. 431-49.

143. Royama, S., and Hamada, K., 'Substitution and Complementarity in the Choice of Risky Assets', in Hester, D.D., and Tobin, J. (eds.), *Risk*

Aversion and Portfolio Choice (New York, J. Wiley, 1967).
144. Ryan, T.M., 'The Demand for Financial Assets by the British Life Funds', *Oxford Bulletin of Economics and Statistics*, vol. 35, no. 1, 1973.
145. Ryan, T.M., 'A Rejoinder', *Oxford Bulletin of Economics and Statistics*, vol. 37, no. 2, 1975, p. 165.
146. Shackle, G.L.S., *Expectation Enterprise and Profit. The Theory of the Firm* (London, Allen and Unwin, 1970).
147. Shedden, A.D., 'A Practical Approach to Applying Immunisation Theory', *Journal of the Institute of Actuaries*, pp. 1-24.
148. Sheppard, D.K., *Growth and Role of UK Financial Institutions, 1880-1962* (London, Methuen, 1971).
149. Shott, F.H., 'Disintermediation Through Policy Loans at Life Insurance Companies', *Journal of Finance*, XXVI, June 1971, pp. 719-29.
150. Sieff, J.A., 'Measuring Investment Performance. The Current Approach', *Financial Analysts Journal*, vol. 22, no. 4, July-August 1966, pp. 93-9.
151. Silber, W.L., *Portfolio Behaviour of Financial Institutions* (New York, Holt, Rinehart and Winston, 1970).
152. Simonson, D.G., 'The Speculative Behaviour of Mutual Funds', *Journal of Finance*, vol. 27, 1972, pp. 381-98.
153. Skerman, R.S., 'A Solvency Standard for Life Assurance Business', *Journal of the Institute of Actuaries*, vol. 92, 1966, pp. 75-84.
154. Smith, P.F., *Economics of Financial Institutions and Markets* (Homewood, Illinois, Irwin, 1971).
155. Society of Investment Analysts, *Portfolio Performance Measurement for Pension Funds*, a working paper, February 1972.
156. Solow, R., *Price Expectations and the Behaviour of the Price Level* (Manchester, Manchester University Press, 1969).
157. Supple, B., *The Royal Exchange Assurance. A History of British Insurance 1720-1970* (Cambridge, Cambridge University Press, 1970).
158. Terrell, W.T., and Fraser, W.J. Jnr., 'Interest Rates, Portfolio Behaviour and Marketable Government Securities', *Journal of Finance*, vol. XXVII, no. 1, March 1972, pp. 1-35.
159. Theil, H., 'Specification Errors and the Estimation of Economic Relationships', *Review of International Statistics*, vol. 25, 1957, pp. 41-51.
160. Theil, H., *Applied Economic Forecasting* (Amsterdam, North Holland, 1966).
161. Tilt, R.R., *Journal of the Institute of Actuaries*, 1914.
162. Titmuss, R.M., *The Irresponsible Society*, Fabian Pamphlet.
163. Tobin, J., and Brainard, W.C., Chapter 3 in Hester, D.D., and Tobin, J. (eds.), *Financial Markets and Economic Activity* (New York, J. Wiley, 1967).
164. Walford, C., 'Insurance Cyclopedia. History of Life Assurance', *Journal of the Institute of Actuaries*, vols. XXV and XXVI, 1889, pp. 207-10.
165. Walker, J.E., *The Investment Process as Characterised by Leading Life Insurance Companies* (Boston: Division of Research, Harvard Business School, 1962).
166. Weaver, D., and Fowler, B.G.H., 'The Assessment of Industrial Ordinary Shares', *Journal of the Institute of Actuaries*, vol. 86, 1960.
167. Wehrle, L.S., 'Life Insurance Investment: The Experience of Four Companies', Chapter 6 in *Studies of Portfolio Behaviour*, Cowles Foundation Monograph 20 (New York, J. Wiley, 1967).
168. Wilson Committee, Committee to review the functioning of financial institutions.
169. Wynn, S., 'Trends in Life Assurance and Related Savings Schemes', *SSRC*,

HR 1826, September 1973.
170. Yaari, M.E., 'On the Consumer's Lifetime Allocation Process', *International Economic Review*, vol. 5, no. 3, September 1964, pp. 304-17.
171. Yaari, M.E., 'Uncertain Lifetime, Life Insurance, and the Theory of the Consumer', *Review of Economic Studies*, 32, no. 2, 1965, pp. 137-50.

INDEX